D1458431

Audley End
Essex

P J Drury   FSA, ARICS
Director, Chelmsford Archaeological Trust

I R Gow   MA
Royal Commission on Ancient and Historical Monuments of Scotland

Edited by M R Apted   MA, PhD, FSA
Formerly Assistant Chief Inspector of Ancient Monuments and Historic Buildings

and Juliet Allan   MA
Inspector of Ancient Monuments and Historic Buildings

LONDON: HER MAJESTY'S STATIONERY OFFICE

Contents

Printed in the UK for HMSO
Dd 737306 C153 7/84 Ed(213880)

ISBN 0 11 671486 7

Historical introduction

Audley End is one of the great country houses of England, standing in its own park, with richly decorated interiors and fine collections of furniture and paintings. But the house as it is today reflects, as do all such houses, the varying tastes and fortunes of its owners in the past—the existing structure, for example, splendid as it is, represents less than half the house as originally built, while internal arrangements and furnishings have been constantly altered by successive generations. The story of Audley End is, therefore, not always easy to follow, and it is further complicated by the need for visitors to follow a route which sometimes means that suites of rooms have to be traversed in the opposite direction to that originally intended. The object of this introduction is to provide a brief summary of the more important points in a complex story.

Audley End stands on the site of the medieval abbey of Walden, granted by Henry VIII in 1538 to Sir Thomas Audley, Speaker of the Parliament responsible for the Dissolution of the Monasteries. Nothing survives above ground of the house which Audley, like many of his contemporaries, created by adapting the monastic buildings to domestic use. Between 1605 and 1614, Audley's grandson, Thomas Howard, Earl of Suffolk and Lord Treasurer to James I, replaced it with the largest Jacobean 'prodigy' house ever built, of which the present Audley End is all that now remains. A palace except in name, Suffolk's house consisted of two courts, the inner, built on the site of the former cloister, containing the Great Hall, Chapel and State Apartments, and the outer, added probably to the designs of John Thorpe, providing lodgings and offices. Formal gardens surrounded the house. Suffolk was also responsible for the stables and a similar row of almshouses, now St Mark's College, south of the Saffron Walden road. (See the plan on page 37.)

Building costs were immense. In 1618, the earl was convicted of embezzlement and, after a brief imprisonment in the Tower, retired in disgrace to Audley End where he died in 1626. His successors were burdened with debt and in 1668 the third earl sold the house to Charles II who was attracted by its proximity to Newmarket and by its palatial disposition. The King's enthusiasm quickly waned and, almost totally neglected after 1688, the house was returned to the Howards in 1701.

The next forty years were ones of desperate retrenchment as successive Earls of Suffolk struggled to reduce the house to a size appropriate to their diminished needs and resources. The sixth earl employed Vanbrugh to pull down most of the now redundant outer court between 1708 and 1713. Next to go, around 1725, were the Jacobean council chamber and chapel projecting from the east range of the inner court, followed by a further reduction of the outer court, leaving only single-storey lodges at the corners of a redesigned forecourt. These changes were accompanied by an unexecuted scheme for grandiose formal gardens, perhaps by the Huguenot architect, Nicholas Dubois. The tenth Earl of Suffolk, the last to live at Audley End, inherited in 1733. He enclosed the Jacobean loggia on the ground floor of the south wing and replanned the first floor to provide new bedroom apartments. On his death, without issue, in 1745, the Suffolk connection ended; the last contents were dispersed at auction and the house stood empty until bought by Elizabeth, Countess of Portsmouth, one of the heirs at law, in 1751.

With the intention of bestowing the property on her recently married soldier nephew, Sir John Griffin Whitwell, the countess set about further replanning the house to make it more suitable to his needs. She demolished the gallery forming the east range of the inner court and replaced it as a means of communication between the truncated north and south wings by a single-storey cloister behind the Great Hall. On inheriting the property in 1762, Sir John Griffin Griffin (as he became) continued his aunt's improvements, remodelling the new cloister to support additional communication galleries on the floors above. He employed Robert Adam to create a fashionable suite of new reception rooms on the ground floor of the south wing and called in 'Capability' Brown to landscape the grounds. New kitchens and offices to Adam's design were also built, and the present chapel fitted up by the joiner, John Hobcraft. Sir John's elevation to the peerage as Baron Howard de Walden in 1784 prompted further works, of which the most important was a magnificent new state apartment on the first floor, created in the hope of receiving the King.

It was Lord Howard's successor Richard Neville, second Lord Braybrooke (1797–1825) who eventually, in 1819, entertained members of the Royal Family at Audley End. He concentrated on consolidating the estate and rebuilt the Saffron Walden lodge. Internal alterations were confined to increasing the comfort and convenience of his predecessor's rooms and it was left to his son, the third Lord Braybrooke (1825–58),

to make the changes by which the house acquired the appearance it largely retains today. These were dictated partly by the third lord's antiquarian enthusiasm, partly by the need to accommodate the large collections of furniture and pictures which both he and his wife, Lady Jane Cornwallis, had inherited and partly by changing domestic tastes. On the first floor, Lord Howard's State Apartment was displaced in favour of a new suite of comfortable and informally furnished reception rooms, while throughout the house Lord Braybrooke and his wife set about reimposing the Jacobean character considered appropriate to an ancestral seat. In the grounds Thomas Rickman rebuilt the lodges in Jacobean style and a formal parterre was laid out to the east of the house.

Lord Braybrooke's three sons who succeeded him in turn between 1858 and 1904 made few further changes. The fourth lord (died 1861), an archaeologist and ornithologist, assembled the notable collection of mounted animals and birds, while his brother the fifth Lord Braybrooke (died 1902) carried out some refurnishing and glazed the lower gallery. Under the sixth lord, the house was let to Lord Howard de Walden and enjoyed something of an Edwardian swansong. Carefully preserved by the seventh Lord Braybrooke (1904–41) until the Second World War, it was then requisitioned by the Government and from 1942–44 served as the headquarters of the Polish section of the Special Operations Executive. Both the eighth lord and his brother died on active service, and in 1948 the house was purchased for the nation out of the Land Fund. Many of the contents, however, remain the property of the present Lord Braybrooke's son, the Honourable Robin Neville, by whose kind permission they are on display.

Tour of the House

Ground floor

The Vestibule or Bucket Hall

This is the screens passage of the Jacobean house, entered from the north porch by a massive oak door carved with an allegory of Peace. It takes its traditional name from the leather fire buckets, painted with the initials and coronet of Richard, third Lord Braybrooke, and the date 1833, which hang from the moulded Jacobean ceiling beams. The Jacobean stone arcade replaces a wooden predecessor, the head of which can still be seen above the stonework on the north side. The north wall was rebuilt around 1725 to provide a fitting entrance to the then new chapel.

The wooden screen has a large central arch, fitted with draught-excluding red baize doors, through which lies the hall. The central opening replaced the usual two side doors in the second Jacobean building phase, the original arrangement being reflected in the design of the screen on the hall side.

The Great Hall

The Great Hall owes its impressive effect to the combination of its ancient decoration and the theatricality of the twin gilded staircases glimpsed through the stone screen. Its present ancient character is deceptive for, although Jacobean in origin, it underwent a thorough restoration by Richard, third Lord Braybrooke, who from 1825 reimposed the Jacobean style on much of the house. His methods can be followed in this room. The finest surviving Jacobean feature is the great oak screen which in the eighteenth century had been painted white. This was stripped to recover its natural, but probably not original, finish. The panelling, which had also been painted, was replaced with new oak stained to match the old, and the ceiling timbers were grained a similar brown to throw them into greater prominence.

Much of the roof is Jacobean, as are the armorial badges in the plaster panels between the beams, but both have been extensively repaired and renewed. Reconstruction in 1687 involved substantial and fairly crude alterations to the hammer-beam brackets, the original form of which is unclear. Among the badges is the crest of Thomas Howard, the builder of Audley End; the remainder are largely of his ancestors or of earlier Earls of Suffolk. The colouring is based on traces found during repairs in 1958.

Although partly old, the chimneypiece was doubled in size by Henry Shaw who did not hesitate to insert a pair of neo-classical statues from the former Adam library into the lower part to give a richer texture. The arms are those of the seventh Earl of Suffolk (1718–22). Although the third lord was critical of the eighteenth century improvements ('For the open screen of stone we are indebted to the bad taste of Sir John Vanbrugh') he was sufficiently aware of its impressive effect to retain it. The lower part of the screen, dating from around 1708, may well be Vanbrugh's design; the upper part was remodelled by Joseph Rose in 1763–64.

View of the interior of the hall c1815 before the third Lord Braybrooke's restoration   RIBA Library

To furnish the hall, Lord Braybrooke collected the Charles II style caned chairs and the other furniture, which includes a Jacobean inlaid buffet. For greater atmosphere he introduced a collection of historic bric-à-brac, like the fine oak carving bought at auction, and the armour. To add a note of colour he had banners with the arms of holders of the manor of Walden placed in the roof. The modernity of the seemingly old-fashioned decoration is characterised by the appearance among the armour of his wife's grandfather's sword. In the same way, the swords and helmets of two sons killed in the Crimea joined those of their ancestors.

The redecorated hall provided a suitable setting for the vast collection of portraits which are thickly hung over every surface except the venerable screen. Only a few are of former owners of Audley End. In a prominent position to the left of the chimneypiece are portraits of Lord Audley and his wife, to whom Walden Abbey had been presented by Henry VIII. Between them is the Duchess of Norfolk, their daughter, who brought the house into the Howard family. These are part of the collection of portraits of sixteenth and seventeenth century owners of the house brought together in the late eighteenth century by Sir John Griffin Griffin. Above them are portraits

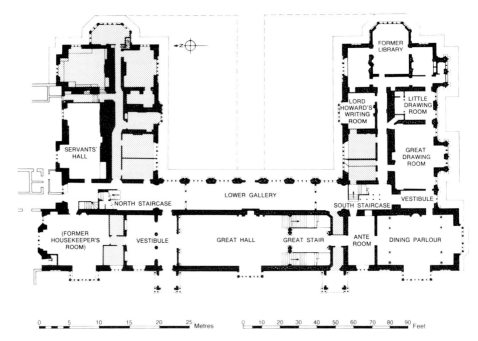

Ground-floor plan of the house as it is now

of the Cornwallis family, which came to Audley End on the third lord's marriage to Lady Jane Cornwallis, eldest daughter and co-heiress of the second Marquess Cornwallis. A third collection of historic portraits was transferred from Billingbear in Berkshire, the Neville seat which Lord Braybrooke had inherited from his father. The sole survivor of the eighteenth-century great hall furniture is the large white marble pedestal in the bay, which Sir John Griffin Griffin bought in 1773 for 95 guineas at the sale of Adam's own art collection then under the hammer to defray his debts on the Adelphi scheme. It was one of the most expensive lots, and its purchase reflects Sir John's gratitude to his architect. John Bearcock supplied a composition statue of Bacchus to stand on it. Nineteenth-century taste substituted the present artificial stone

group which Sir John bought from Mrs Coade in 1772.

The Great Stair

The Great Stair, like the Great Hall, retains its Jacobean ceiling, but the appearance of both was changed when the windows that lit them on the east were blocked in the eighteenth century. The staircase itself, the arch on the ground floor now leading to the Great Apartments, and the saloon doorcase on the first floor, were probably designed by Nicholas Dubois, *c*1725. The Doric columns flanking the doorways are reused Jacobean work, probably derived from the concurrent demolition of the original Chapel, whose interior had been 'very sumptuous with marble pillars.'

The stairwell contains two large cases of

shells and fossils collected by the fourth Lord Braybrooke from boyhood. Under that on the léft is a fossilised mammoth's tusk which caused great excitement when it was discovered near the house in 1832.

The Great Apartments

The next seven rooms have been restored as far as possible to their appearance in the early 1770s. Where original items of furniture are missing, they have been replaced in accordance with descriptions in surviving records.

Replanning in 1736 had involved the conversion of the first floor, designed as the principal floor, into bedroom apartments. On the ground floor of the south wing, a suite of irregular, awkwardly connected public rooms was contrived. Sir John Griffin

Plans of the ground floor of the south range of the inner court c1770 and c1835

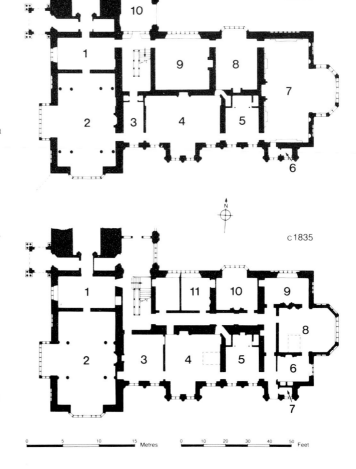

1 Ante Room
2 Dining Parlour
3 Vestibule
4 Great Drawing Room
5 Little Drawing Room
6 Water Closet
7 Library
8 Sir John's Writing Room
9 Supper Parlour
10 Arcade

1 Tapestry Room
2 Summer Dining Parlour
3 State Dressing Room
4 State Bedroom
5 Lady's State Dressing Room
6 Lady's Dressing Room
7 Water Closet
8 Red Bedroom
9 Gentlemen's Dressing Room
10 Lady's Maid's Room for State Apartment
11 Valet's Room for State Apartment

Griffin, on inheriting, asked Robert Adam to recast the suite which had been further reduced by Lady Portsmouth. Although little could be done with the basic structure, Adam was able by moving partitions, flues and doorways to create a series of individually regular rooms centred on a new Great Drawing Room in the south front overlooking the flower garden. The defects gave way to a theatrical scenery of vistas, columns and niches which made a virtue from necessity. Rooms like these show how Adam fused his architectural skills with his wider interest in the 'art of living' (his own phrase) to produce an architecture of pleasure tailored for fashionable entertaining. As well as the dinner which formed the basis of such a party, guests were regaled with an aesthetic banquet of contrasting shapes, colours and decoration as they moved through the suite in stages.

The plasterwork is by Joseph Rose, the carving and gilding by William and Robert Adair, and the drawing room furniture by Gordon and Tait who supervised the fitting up of the rooms.

The Ante Room The Ante Room formed part of the processional route to the Great Drawing Room. Guests would have been conducted through a new door in the east wall designed by Adam to line up with the doorways of the north parlours. The original door, now a cupboard, was left as a dummy, and the room was given a new cornice. The all-white scheme repeated that of the Great Hall at the time. The Ante Room was used to store furniture belonging to the dining parlour. Tables for eight, ten and sixteen guests were kept here until required as were four extra chairs to make up sixteen. The modern table is similar to the one made for the dining parlour by John Cobb. The 'brass

half bells to hold doors open' are listed in the 1797 inventory. The double doors to the dining parlour were introduced *c*1830.

The Dining Parlour Eighteenth-century guests would have approached the Dining Parlour from the Great Drawing Room and Vestibule. Today visitors enter from the service end through one of the columnar screens introduced to disguise the irregularities of the room. The apparent symmetry is an illusion as the screens are at different distances from the end walls. Dinner was served early in the afternoon and the 'pea-green' decoration picked out in white was designed to lead the eye out across the lawns of Brown's landscape.

Adam recommended a hard finish for dining rooms on practical grounds: 'Instead of being hung with damask, tapestry etc they are always finished with stucco and adorned with statues and paintings, that

Plan and interior elevations of the Dining Parlour, drawn by Placido Columbani

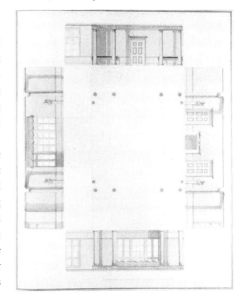

they may not retain the smell of the victuals.' In this case, however, festoon curtains were used to disguise variations in the form of the two windows. Although placed at different heights they were maintained at the same level by balance weights. Modern curtains replace the originals which were made of 'pea-green lutestring,' a glossy silk. Statuary was unsuitable in such a low room, and so Sir John commissioned four alabaster vases from Francis Harwood, which were fitted inside with candle-sockets so that they could be used to light the room dramatically in winter. Only one now survives, from which the others have been copied. Variations on this theme recur throughout the room: the chimneyboard which hid the grate in summer, one of five painted by Biagio Rebecca for the Great Apartments, depicts a large urn, while a further vase, painted white, was erected in the garden outside to close the vista through the south bay.

The mahogany furniture was inherited from Lady Portsmouth. Two white marble sideboards stand behind the columns of the service end. The ten side and two arm chairs reupholstered in green leather by Gordon and Tait are no longer at the house and the existing chairs shown are a mixed set collected for the upstairs dining room c1920. Two small 'Florence vases' stand on the chimneypiece (that on the right is a reproduction). To complete its ornaments, Mr Evans of Derby made the 'large petrification column' in 1776 and a 'pair of large obelisks' in blue john which have since disappeared.

Dinner was served with great ceremony. Sir John's widow warned her successor, who was about to move to Audley End, that he would find hardly any china since 'we used only plate.' The remark conveys a little of the splendour of this meal, with crested silver, a procession of liveried servants and (on special occasions) a band playing in the great hall. After dessert the ladies left by the door to the right of the chimneypiece, thus avoiding the service end. This convenient exit was first designed as a concealed door or jib but was altered in 1785 to match the entrance from the Ante Room.

The Vestibule Visitors passed through the Vestibule, finished in stucco painted 'Naples yellow and dead white,' on their way from the Ante Room to the Drawing Room and thence to the Dining Parlour. Adam designed a pair of richly decorated pedestals to support lamps which, in 1786, were moved to the State Dressing Room; simpler modern copies preserve the formality. Until 1826 the present window was a glazed door leading to the flower garden.

The Great Drawing Room The Great Drawing Room, where guests were received by their host and hostess, was the grandest in the suite and is richly gilded to suit its importance. The ceiling is only 11ft 6in (3.5m) high and the humble dimensions challenged Adam's skill. He scaled down every element so that the dado, the woodwork with its delicate enrichments, and the furniture are all smaller than those of an average room. The chimneypiece, of sienna and carrara marble, was made by John Moore. For the ceiling Adam chose a selection of his favourite neo-classical motifs, but its framework of strong diagonals enclosing triple 'domes' follows the plan of the room, while the paired griffins play on his client's name and reveal the architect's engaging professional manner.

The other decorations reflect the ceiling ornaments but it is the choice of silk that establishes the character of the room. It may seem surprising that Adam approved the florid crimson, green, and white damask but it is also found in his other houses. A small-scale pattern was chosen. The ceiling was tinted to harmonise with the silk (the original 1771 paintwork by John Wateridge survives in the bay) and the woodwork, decorated in the same colours. The upholstery and curtains were of the same silk. The sofa backs were designed to fit the pattern exactly and the chairs were upholstered to suit the sofas. In the usual eighteenth-century manner the furniture was arranged against the walls, leaving the centre of the room free. Because the dado was unusually low, the seat backs lay against the walls which were hung so that the pattern ran through unbroken, locking each piece of furniture tightly into the overall pattern. The chairs on the end walls stand so close to the tables that the latter have concave ends to receive them. The dazzling unity of the original scheme was lost in the 1962 restoration when the silk was rewoven but is verified by early photographs.

Pier glasses, normally sited between windows, are placed on the end walls where they set up infinite reflections. The glasses were supplied by Gordon and Tait but their frames were carved by the Adairs. Adam made full-sized coloured designs for pier tables with scagliola tops, but only his design for the tops was used and they were modified to marquetry. The tables were French polished c1890 but slight traces remain of the original red, grey-blue, green, and pink dyes which match the ceiling. Each table originally supported a blue john and ormolu 'Bingley vase' candleabra supplied by Boulton and Fothergill, complemented by porcelain set out on the chimneypiece and tables. The present vases are modern. The carpet now in the South Library upstairs may be the one originally in this room.

The effect of such a room depended on preventing the colours fading. The seat furniture had peagreen and white linen covers and the tables, leather covers. Paper and canvas covers protected the wall hangings when the room was not in use. Adjustable green-painted venetian blinds, now replaced by modern copies, were installed in 1777 to keep out the sun.

The Little Drawing Room   The Little Drawing Room was to divert the ladies while the gentlemen lingered in the Dining Parlour. The Great Drawing Room was expressed in the conventional terms which etiquette demanded. This room, which had a less exacting brief, dispenses even with a chimneypiece to produce one of the most vivid evocations of the 'rage for the antique' in England.

Its elaborate articulation and screened sofa-niche are present in Adam's drawing of October 1764, although this design was modified in execution. For an early scheme that was to have a chimneypiece, Adam supplied 'A design of a Ceiling in the Taste of the Painting of the Ancients.' Although not carried out, its *grotesque* decoration was the germ of this 'Painted Room.' Sir John commissioned Biagio Rebecca to decorate the 'mosaic' ceiling and panels. Rebecca was too able a designer to follow Adam's suggestions slavishly and in place of the intended ceiling roundel showing a flying griffin bearing Cupid, he evolved 'Jupiter at the request of Venus dispatching Mercury to dispose Dido in favour of Aeneas and the Trojans.' The feigned bas reliefs are derived from Montfaucon's publications of ancient sculpture, but the long panel over the alcove is his own composition.

The walls were painted to harmonise with the wall paintings and reflect the colours of

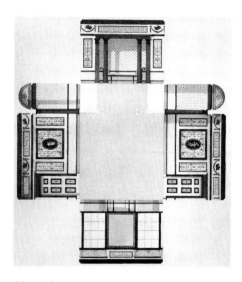

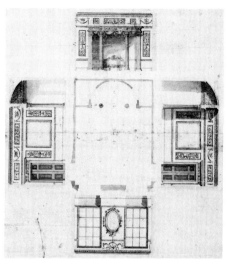

Plan and interior elevations of the Little Drawing Room by Placido Columbani

Design for the Little Drawing Room by Robert Adam

the adjoining room. Of the furnishings, only the curtains survive in the original silk. The large couch is of exceptional quality and sufficient of the gilding remains to show how this glitteringly metallic finish must have successfully mimicked the bronze furniture of antiquity. A diminutive pair of couches and four matching stools were designed to fit precisely below the panelling. This precious suite had two sets of covers, one of blue and white silk, and another of white flannel. One couch has disappeared but the elegant glass-topped table in its place was recorded here in 1797. The square pier glass designed by Adam was made by the Adairs in 1771. The pier table originally supported another candle-vase by Boulton and Fothergill decorated with griffins, which may also have been a perfume burner. The 'very fine Tapestry Carpet Apple Green Ground' made by Moore in 1773 to complete this feminine room no longer survives.

'The art of living' demanded a compromise with the 'art of architecture' in one final change when Lady Griffin Griffin had the columns reset further apart to admit her hooped evening dress to the alcove.

The Library The Adam Library was destroyed in 1825 when a new Library was created in the same position on the floor above. The ceiling was lowered and partitions were inserted to form a bedroom apartment and corridor. To display the surviving fragments and to show how Adam terminated the Drawing Room enfilade, a modern *trompe l'œil* has been painted by Alan Powers. One of Adam's temple-like bookcases has been restored to its original position and stocked with some of the books he had specially rebound in scarlet and gold chequers.

The Library Exhibition The Library served as a grand sitting room where the party,

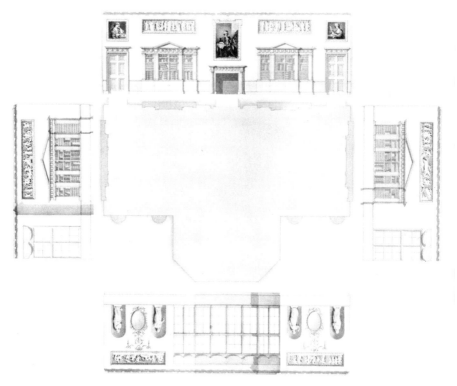

Plan and interior elevations of the Library by Placido Columbani

reunited on the return of the gentlemen, gathered over the card tables and took tea or coffee. Adam rebuilt the bay window to take advantage of the vista over the Home Park. Ceiling and walls were painted cream picked out in white which contrasted with the preceding rooms and showed to advantage a group of specially commissioned works of art. Cipriani was paid £315 for his cycle of six grisaille friezes depicting the elements and the arts and sciences, of which two are now shown by courtesy of the Saffron Walden Museum. Rebecca provided a chimneyboard with a painted altar, also on display, to match the friezes. Benjamin West's portraits of Sir John and his two wives which formerly hung here are now in the South Library. The four niches contained statues of vestals and sybils modelled by Bacon and made in Mrs Coade's patent stone. Two were incorporated in the Great Hall chimneypiece in 1830; the casts displayed here were taken in 1981.

Sir John reused some of his aunt's furniture including a sofa, six 'French elbow' chairs and ten stools, recovered with needlework and brass-nailed. Two three-drawered pier tables were provided in 1766 to match the earlier library table. The blend of comfort and magnificence was conveyed on the one hand by a very fine glass chandelier and by a fitted Brussels carpet in 'crimson shades' on the other.

The model is intended to help visitors to

imagine the original appearance of the library. A collection of views of the house and park by William Tomkins painted in the 1780s is displayed in part of the former library. The estate accounts confirm that the details shown are painted with photographic accuracy, probably with the aid of a *camera obscura*.

Sir John's Writing Room The 1825–28 service corridor has reduced the size of the north parlours which played a subsidiary role in the Great Apartments. The larger was a supper parlour (not open to the public), while the smaller room provided a study or writing room where Sir John could attend to his political and county business in private. When the family were alone the two rooms provided a sitting room and private dining room.

Both rooms were decorated to display the fine collection of cabinet pictures which Sir John purchased at auction, being hung with 'blue paper' bordered with gold fillet to show off the gold frames. The curtains were of matching blue lutestring; the shade of the modern replacement in the writing room is based on a surviving fragment. Several of the pictures on display were here in 1797; the others hung in the supper parlour. The corridor has been redecorated in its early nineteenth-century colours.

The South Stair

The South Stair of the original Jacobean house became in later years the best staircase leading to the guests' bedrooms. It was painted white in the eighteenth century, and has been reconstructed on several occasions to suit changes in the layout of the floors which it serves. The paint was stripped in 1823, and later, to give it more importance, heraldic beasts were added to the newel

posts. The third Lord Braybrooke carried out repairs and replaced missing ornament in moulded composition.

The General Prospect of the Royal Palace of Audlyene which hangs at the foot of the stair is by Henry Winstanley, c1676.

The huge painting by Jan Griffier the younger opposite the stair shows the entrance front of Billingbear in Berkshire (demolished 1926), with Windsor Castle in the distance, c1738. Painted for Lady Portsmouth's London house, which she also left to her nephew, it came to Audley End in 1778.

The Lower Gallery

The Lower Gallery was an open arcade overlooking the 1830s flower garden until 1863 when it was 'enclosed and taken into the house' by R C Hussey for the fifth Lord Braybrooke. It echoes the abbey cloister which was on this site. The basic stonework came from the loggia on the east side of the inner court of the Jacobean house which Lady Portsmouth had re-erected in single-storey form on this side, to link the two wings of her reduced house. After 1762 it was carefully dismantled by her nephew and rebuilt further from the hall wall, to support a pair of communication galleries on the floors above.

The arcade was glazed to house part of the growing collection of mounted birds which had been the especial enthusiasm of the fourth lord. His interest in ornithology may have been stimulated by the 'Menagerie' founded by Sir John in the early 1770s. This contained exotic song birds and survived until the 1890s.

The North Stair

The North Stair has a similar history to that on the south side. The second-best stair in the Jacobean house, it took on the character of a private backstair to the family rooms on the upper floors of the north wing after 1752 when the ground floor was given over to the offices.

First Floor

The North Lobby

The original position of the stair is indicated by the two huge doorcases introduced after the house returned to the Suffolks in the early eighteenth century. Around 1736 the flights were narrowed to give access to one of the outer bedroom apartments formed by the division of the rooms in the north wing. The present lobby was formed in 1763 when Sir John Griffin Griffin added the first bay of his new communication

gallery to the existing staircase landing in order to light it.

The space is dominated by one of the marble-topped radiator cases installed with the 1843 heating system. The small longcase clock stands in the place formerly occupied by a dwarf longcase clock purchased by Sir John. From it he ran the house with such military precision that his sister-in-law complained in a letter that 'we run by clockwork here.' At the entrance to the gallery are two of the early bird cases unaffected by the later rearrangement, and a pair of portraits in rococo frames brought from the London house in 1778.

The North Wing

In the Jacobean house the first floor of the north wing contained the State Apartment

First-floor plan of the house as it is now

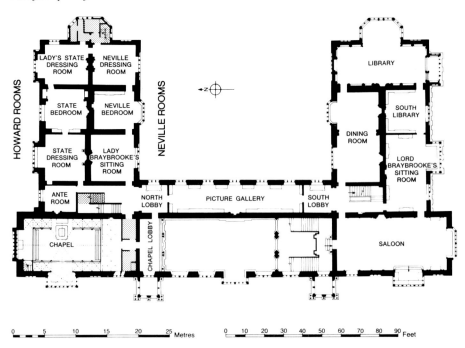

TOUR OF THE HOUSE

probably intended for the Queen. The original layout is shown in the reconstruction plan on page 52, which also indicates the surviving Jacobean ceilings and friezes. They are one of the chief glories of the house. The plasterers worked in very low relief and had such a keen sense of line that their work is more akin to drawing than sculpture. The feathers of birds and veining of leaves are realistically modelled, and all has a crispness hardly dulled by many coats of whitening. Later alterations copy the original designs, but in bright sunshine they are clearly distinguishable.

Around 1708 the large Jacobean windows were reduced in height and the friezes extended across them, the bold three-dimensional modelling of the fruit, in particular, reflecting current taste. The conversion of the original rooms into the two existing bedroom apartments, which took place around 1736, involved the division of the Jacobean withdrawing chamber and bedchamber. The plasterwork of the associated friezes is flat, imprecise and of a very poor standard compared with the earlier work.

The Jacobean state rooms had tapestries below the deep friezes. After the 1736 alterations the rooms were panelled, and in 1763 the bolection mouldings were cut off to allow the rooms to be wallpapered. In general the Jacobean oak chimneypieces were retained because they harmonised with the plasterwork. The fireplaces were reduced in size by slips of Derbyshire limestone, reused from the Jacobean house.

Sir John Griffin Griffin took the north suite as his own after 1762. The south-facing apartment was used by family guests until

Right: Comparative details of plasterwork in the first-floor friezes

c1605–14

c1708

c1736

1826 when the third lord moved there because of its sunnier outlook.

Since much of the original furniture of these rooms has been retained by the family, they are now used to display the former contents of the two bedroom apartments in the south wing, destroyed in the third Lord Braybrooke's early nineteenth-century alterations.

The State Apartment

In 1784 Sir John achieved his ambition when his claim to the ancestral Barony of Howard de Walden was recognised by George III. He immediately began the series of alterations in the south wing in order to create a magnificent State Apartment for the reception of the King. The surviving contents of this apartment, including the state bed, are now displayed in the rooms on the north side of the north wing.

The State Dressing Room Furnishings fit for the King had to be even more splendid than the drawing room furniture. The basis of the State Apartment furnishings was the portrait of George II by Pine, purchased by Lord Howard in 1784 and now in the Dining Room. To partner it, he commissioned the copy of Gainsborough's full length of George III, now on the west wall, from William Hanneman. They were placed in enriched broad gold frames made by James Gough. The portraits of the Duke of Brunswick (who married George III's sister) and Prince Ferdinand were copied by Joseph Parker from pictures in the collection of General Fawcett. Lord Howard had served under both princes in Germany.

The rooms of the original State Apartment were hung by the supervising upholsterers Chipchase and Lambert with a watered blue silk dyed to match the Chinese silk of the state bed. This has been simulated here in paint as it was not thought desirable to hang these rooms with silk; they were always papered. The fillet round the feigned hangings is the original 'broad hollow mould' in gilt French grey and scarlet made by Prusserot. A matching curtain of modern tabby has been made on a surviving pulley board. The original was trimmed with elaborate French grey and gold fringes like those on the state bed. The large cloak pins have been copied from two which survive.

The voluptuous English mahogany bombe commode is one of a pair which Lord Howard probably inherited from his aunt. The pedestals, designed by Adam in 1765 for the vestibule, were equipped with small platforms to take a pair of lustres probably from the library; the present lustres are modern. The King's dressing and writing tables have not been traced. In September 1786 Lord Howard purchased from Josiah Wedgwood the 'Large Ornamental vase apotheosis of Homer' and '2 Antique Ewers sacred to Bacchus' to serve as chimney ornaments; their blue jasper complimented the silk. One ewer has been lost.

Items added to the Dressing Room after 1786 include the 'very elegant Pole stand richly carved in white and gold with a neat vase' and the 'mother of Pearl backgammon table,' recorded in the 1797 inventory of the original room. The washstand, one of a pair, has ormolu mounts similar to the commode and was added to the suite *c*1830.

The inventory includes no chairs for this room, possibly reflecting royal etiquette which forbade anyone to sit in the King's presence. A set of stuffed chairs upholstered in the same blue silk were kept in an ante room to be brought in when required.

Right: The state bed

The State Bedroom The Howard de Walden state bed (page 19), made by Chipchase and Lambert in 1786, is the most important piece of furniture in the house. It is also one of the most complete surviving beds of its period. Its designer is unknown but it is possible that Rebecca may have been involved.

The complex history of the hangings was revealed when the bed was repaired in 1977 under the auspices of the Victoria and Albert Museum. Although the flowers appear to be embroidered onto the blue silk, they are in fact appliquéd with overstitching in the same colours. Mr J Seneschal was paid for this work in June 1786. The embroideries are actually worked on a heavy cream silk from which they have been cut. A later nineteenth-century account claims that they came from a court dress belonging to Lady Portsmouth. Certainly contemporary court dresses and trains have comparable embroidery and the variety of stitches with which the silver gilt threads are worked seem better suited to a moving surface where they would sparkle than flattened out on the bed. If true, it was a singular act of piety by Lord Howard to the aunt to whom he owed his fortune and the house. The source proved insufficient for the whole because the dome is decorated with Chinese embroideries on paper. Originally the curtains would have been elaborately furled to display the white enamelled footposts, but the silk is now too fragile to permit this. The blue paint was added to freshen up the frame *c*1890.

The bed stands in an impressive bed alcove, probably created *c*1736 and later widened. The ceiling is part of a larger Jacobean one. The chimneypiece, from the original state dressing room, was placed here *c*1828 in part exchange for the oak surround now in the library.

Hanneman's companion copy of Gainsborough's *Queen Charlotte* has place of honour over the chimneypiece, as in the original room where a similarly framed glass hung over the other mahogany commode, now missing, opposite the bed. On either side of the bed are a pair of night tables with front panels which slide like sashes instead of doors and which matched the commode. The two white enamelled chairs were made by Francis Gilding to take gilt embroideries. One of the original four unusually shaped stools has been restored by kind permission of the Honorable Robin Neville.

The Lady's State Dressing Room This was one of the new interior dressing rooms that Lord Howard added to the four bedroom apartments by building above Lady Portsmouth's single storey pavilions in 1785. In the other apartments they served as ladies' dressing rooms, a plan that also provided back stairs, ladies' maids' rooms and water closets in the deep new bays and was luxurious by the standards of the day. Lord Howard, however, preferred to use this as his own Dressing Room as it gave him easy access to his other dressing room on the ground floor, via the back stairs behind the east door. The lower room was situated near the offices as in most landowner's houses, so that he could interview people whom he would not wish to admit to the rest of the house. As it is a man's dressing room this room has the simplest of the ceilings designed for the four new rooms by the plasterer Joseph Rose.

The room is now furnished as the Lady's State Dressing Room. Although fit for the Queen, its furnishings could be less formal and more fashionable, as it was necessarily very private. In fitting up the room Lord Howard at last found a use for the two panels of Soho tapestry, woven by Paul Saunders, ordered over twenty years previously for a discarded scheme for the great apartments. To make them fit the room, Rebecca painted extensions of the two scenes on coarse canvas to simulate tapestry. After conservation, the tapestries will be hung in this room.

Most of the original furniture of the Lady's State Dressing Room, including a set of black japanned seat furniture, a large satinwood commode fitted as a dressing table, and a writing table with silk firescreen, is no longer at the house. The present furniture includes a set of eight oval-backed chairs made for the Lady's Dressing Room of the Red Apartment, the other ormolu-mounted washstand and a daybed covered in pink damask made for the suite in the nineteenth century. Festoon curtains and chair covers have been made from the same material. The original dressing room had a fitted carpet, and the Brussels one now shown here is from the nineteenth-century Red Apartment on the ground floor. The curious 'panel of needlework in a gilt frame' is mentioned in the 1797 inventory.

The chimney ornaments, of blue jasper, are suited to a lady's room and consist of an 'altar flower pot (The Seasons) and 2 Grecian Figure Candleabras.' The oval pier glasses were unusually mounted on the doors of the powdering closet and its balancing dummy. These were made into a wardrobe in the nineteenth century and were placed in this bay in 1979.

The Neville Dressing Room

When the third lord moved to the south apartment he took this room as his dressing room, and Lady Jane had the outer room. Its elaborate ceiling was intended for a lady's dressing room. The rooms were hung with portraits of members of the family and close friends. The wall paper is a modern copy of that chosen for the suite c1830.

The room is furnished with a miscellaneous collection of furniture. The large inlaid seventeenth century Dutch armoire, fitted with wardrobe trays, is one of the pieces acquired by the Braybrookes in Antwerp on their trip to the Low Countries in 1828. The four vases on the chimneypiece were painted by Lady Jane's mother, Louisa, Marchioness Cornwallis.

The Neville Bedroom

The Neville Bedroom has its original ceiling and a particularly interesting Jacobean frieze with heads in high relief. Its narrowness, which contrasts with all the others in the house, may be due to its having been designed to accommodate specific tapestry hangings. The red bed was made by Paul Saunders in 1766 for the second best bedroom apartment in the south wing. The footposts and later the sprung base were added when it was moved to the ground floor. The lacquer furniture and shaped glass in its gilt frame have always accompanied the red bed. The huge fitted mahogany wardrobe whose panels follow those of the doors was, like others throughout the house, added by the third Lord Braybrooke.

Lady Braybrooke's Sitting Room

This room has the southern half of the Jacobean ceiling first seen in the State Dressing Room. The oak chimneypiece may have come from the ground floor as it is lower than those in other first-floor rooms. Much of the furniture in this room until 1939 was purchased from Lord Braybrooke in 1980. This made it possible to recreate the appearance of the room as recorded by the photographer Bedford Lemere in 1891.

Lady Braybrooke's Sitting Room,
photographed in 1891 by Bedford Lemere
National Monuments Record

The underlying structure of the furniture is Lady Jane's. Like many of her contemporaries she was attracted by richly mounted French furniture. For her own dressing room she selected the two Louis XV corner cupboards which are signed by Flechy. A commode by Ellaume is of the same period and has a similar marble slab. The armoire inlaid with flowers, later fitted with wardrobe trays, is signed by Carel. These were partnered by a group of oval portraits of her children, prints of relations and friends,

22 AUDLEY END HOUSE

TOUR OF THE HOUSE

rooms. In the foreground of the photograph can be seen one of the best of these pieces, a very fine dressing table like one in the Royal Collection.

The richness of effect was increased by juxtaposing contrasting styles and it was at this time that the sixteenth century French oak armoire, the second of those bought in 1828, was moved here. A variety of textiles and ceramics completed this lively room. In the twentieth century, it became the family's private sitting room. The striking carpet was made in India before the Second World War to replace that in the photograph which had worn out.

Visitors return to the north lobby which they cross to enter the chapel

The Chapel Lobby

It was probably Adam who had the idea of using the Jacobean music gallery over the screens passage as the dramatic new entrance to the Chapel. The Jacobean chapel had been demolished *c*1725, and a new chapel formed in the north wing by removing the floor of the northern Great Chamber to provide a two-storied room entered from the ground floor. A small portion of the floor was retained to form a gallery for the family at the south end, entered from the stair landing. After 1762 Adam replaced the rest of the floor (but at a lower level) creating a housekeeper's room on the ground floor, with the existing Chapel above.

The lobby was appropriately hung with religious pictures and a print of the east window of King's College Chapel, Cambridge.

The Chapel

The family and staff gathered in the Chapel for morning prayers during the week. On

and light modern dressing room furniture.

By 1891 the effect had become infinitely richer. Lady (Florence) Braybrooke rescued much of Lord Howard's furniture from attics and servant's bedrooms. It was french polished and reupholstered in stamped plush by William Robson, the local house furnisher in Saffron Walden, and set out in the principal

Sunday they processed to Saffron Walden Church. Although conceived in 1768 and completed in 1772 at the same time as the Great Apartments, it was designed not by Adam but John Hobcraft, a successful joiner. Hobcraft's men made all the furnishings which are remarkably complete. The result is pure carpenter's 'Gothick,' a free-standing structure of timber, lath, and plaster. Much of the Jacobean ceiling remains in place above the vaults, pierced by the struts which support them. The woodwork and vault were painted to imitate stone. A realistic pavement in squares of 'Portland and Bremen' stone was simulated by a huge oilcloth supplied in three pieces by Nathan Smith; the present floor-covering is a modern replacement. The windows of painted glass were made by William Peckitt of York to Rebecca's designs. 'Our Saviours Last Supper' (1771) is depicted over the altar while the (liturgical) north transept originally contained the 'Offering of the Easter Magi' (1772). The glass now in this window comes from Chicksands Priory.

The unusual plan proved remarkably well adapted to its function and nicely observed the hierarchic gradations of society. The altar and preacher's chair were raised above the nave. The table had a purple velvet cover fringed in gold. The chair, upholstered in the same materials, is made of olive wood and was carved by Sefferin Alken. Sir John was shocked by its cost, but Hobcraft explained that this material took three times longer to work than other woods because of its cross grain. The family were accommodated in a luxurious seat in the form of a tribune with its own chimneypiece and a Wilton carpet to match that inside the altar rail; the present carpet is a modern replacement. The individual Gothick chairs, when not in use, were ranged against the panelling into which they fit exactly. In use they were

Late eighteenth-century view of Chapel looking towards the Gallery

pulled forward to the front of the seat. Their leather upholstery, the hassocks and the book cushions were red. The indoor servants sat in the organ gallery over the family seat, reached by its own stairs. This was closed in after 1826. The kitchen and outdoor staff, who entered by a staircase on the left of the altar, sat in the aisles on plain oak benches and had brown leather kneelers.

The half-size model for Rossi's Cornwallis tomb in St Paul's Cathedral, presented to Lord Braybrooke in 1835, stood originally in the chapel gallery.

The New Reception Rooms

The next six rooms are the third Lord Braybrooke and Lady Jane's reception rooms which replaced the Great Apartments on the ground floor after 1825. They were to form a setting for the three picture collections, three libraries and three sets of family relics. The style is Jacobean throughout. Where there were no surviving ceilings and friezes, copies were supplied. The supervising upholsterers were Dowbigging and the main colour used throughout was red. The principal contents are antique French furniture, although the dining room was in plain mahogany. The seat furniture was chosen for comfort and, if not upholstered in chintz loose covers, has needlework by the ladies. There was no fear in the new rooms, as Lord Howard's sister-in-law found in the old, 'of so much state wanting to be kept up that I lived in fear of spoiling everything I touched.'

The Picture Gallery   The gallery was added by Sir John Griffin Griffin in 1762 to provide communication between the north and south wings. Joseph Rose's 'Jacobean' fret ceiling suggests that it was conceived as a reflection of the original long gallery which had closed the court to the east. It was simply furnished, and was used for the family to assemble in before morning prayers.

The third lord redecorated it to bring it into his suite of reception rooms by adding shields to the cornice, carvings to the door frames, and wood graining over the white paint. The chimneypiece is not from the Jacobean house and must have been specially acquired by Lord Braybrooke; an Elizabethan bed-head seems the most likely source of its upper part.

The redecorated gallery provided a suitable setting for the long run of Cornwallis family portraits. From the similarity of their framing they must, with the full lengths in the Great Hall, once have formed a Georgian gallery at Brome Hall, Suffolk, a Cornwallis seat. They now play second fiddle to the fourth Lord Braybrooke's bird collection, which was remounted *c*1860.

The chairs, which may be from Sir John's gallery, are of a type often used in such a room. The curtains date from 1900, but the striped blinds are earlier and were used throughout the house from the early nineteenth century. The modern carpet laid along both gallery and lobbies reproduces the mottled Brussels carpet fitted when the new cases were installed. The large collection of ceramics, mainly Chinese, has been added to since 1830.

The South Lobby   The south lobby was given its own special character by the five Lely portraits originally at Billingbear, which hang here. It can have been no easy task for the third Lord Braybrooke and Lady Jane to fit the collections from three country houses into one. The panache with which they did so is well demonstrated here.

The Dining Room   The Dining Room strikingly demonstrates the different approaches

Mid-nineteenth-century watercolour of the Dining Room

of Sir John and the third lord to their suites of reception rooms. Sir John was concerned solely with the overall effect. Here the third lord was so anxious to preserve the ceilings of the bedroom and dressing room from which the new Dining Room was created that he even managed to retain the original friezes above the former partition. He introduced a matching pair of chimneypieces made of old parts, but was clearly uninterested in producing a unified interior.

The impressive Jacobean ceiling of the western compartment, like that of its equivalent in the north wing, was cut in two when the fireplace wall was inserted c1736. The sections of original frieze contain roundels representing America on the east and Europe on the west. That on the south is a copy of 'America.'

The room has ample wall space for hanging the full-length portraits. *George II*, still in the state apartment frame, was placed at the east end. Pine described it as 'universally allowed to be the most like of any in being.' It was balanced on the west by Beechey's portrait of the great Marquess Cornwallis.

The comfortable stuffed dining chairs by Dowbigging, originally upholstered with green leather, the plush curtains and the Axminster carpet are contemporary with the alterations; a Turkey carpet was the conventional choice for dining rooms.

One of the sideboards and the sectioned dinner table are earlier in style and may have been made for the second Lord Braybrooke's Eating Room (formerly the Adam Dining Parlour) c1810. The second sideboard was made to match when they were brought upstairs. If sections of the table were not in use, they were, like the smaller oval table for a few diners, pushed into the inside corners and the bay.

The tablecloth bears Cornwallis inventory marks. The desert service is Sévres. The third lord collected seventeenth-century plate to display in this room.

The Library The Library was formed out of the lady's dressing rooms of the Red and State Apartments. Since they were additions of 1785 they contained no early features. With the help of Henry Shaw and Henry Harrison, the third lord 'carefully imitated the individual elements' of its scheme 'from examples in different parts of the house' so that the new Library harmonised with the adjoining rooms. The ceiling design was copied from the western part of the adjoining Dining Room and the frieze from the South Library. The pilastered panelling in the Saloon provided a convenient precedent for modern adjustable bookcases, made by Bennett and Hunt. The chimneypiece was taken from what is now the State Bedroom.

This was the family's sitting room when they were alone, perhaps on account of its splendid view. The furniture and its arrangement are very different from those of Adam's Library. The large Louis XV library table in the bay suited the magnificent new decorations. In the centre of the room is a round table where members of the family or guests could sit and work. Further out are a set of comfortable rather than elegant chairs and sofas covered in simple chintz. That on the left of the chimneypiece has the original chintz cover chosen for the room by Lady Jane *c*1830. Across the front of the sofa is a conveniently placed table. The room has a fitted Brussels carpet. In winter, the curtains, now modern replacements, could be hung on rods across the bays for greater warmth.

The black japanned table with ivory knobs was specially designed to hold and display the huge scrapbook assembled by the second lord in 1809 to contain a large collection of engravings of past owners of the mansion, with views and architectural drawings of the house.

The South Library From 1786–1825, this was the State Bedroom and represents about half of the Jacobean King's Bedchamber, which was severed when the house was reduced by the Countess of Portsmouth so that the Jacobean ceiling is now asymmetrical. The frieze on the east wall was executed by William Wilton in 1753; of all the copies of Jacobean work, his is the most faithful to both design and spirit.

The third Lord Braybrooke moved Adam's bedroom chimneypiece to its present position and refitted the room to accommodate topographical books. The cases have an adjustable shelving system quite different from that in the adjoining Library, and may have been made for the second Lord Braybrooke *c*1810, to replace Adam's elegant but not very capacious cases in the ground-floor Library. The sabre-legged chair which adapts to form a set of library steps was probably purchased at the same time. The upper parts of the cases were added subsequently.

The new arrangement provided a fitting home for Benjamin West's portraits of Sir John Griffin Griffin and his two wives, displaced from Adam's Library. West acquitted himself of the delicate task of painting the two wives with perfect tact. Anna Maria, above the east door, who died in 1764, is depicted as a sybil after Domenichino; her music is a sacred song, just readable as *Domino confide* ('Trust in the Lord'). Katherine, whom Sir John married in 1765, also poses as a sybil, after Guecino.

This room was too small to act as more than a connecting link in the suite but was an appropriate place to display the family's most precious relics. The most celebrated is the sixteenth-century walnut armchair, bearing a plate which records that 'This chair once the property of Alexander Pope, was given as a keepsake to the nurse who attended him in his last illness. From her descendants it was obtained by Reverend Thomas Ashley, when Curate of the Parish of Binfield, and kindly presented by him to Lord Braybrooke in 1844. . . .'

The present curtains are of c1900, but they replace the most spectacular relic of all, the red Italian silk damask material woven with the Neville saltire and initial which had been presented in 1670 to a Neville ancestor by Cosimo de' Medici, Grand Duke of Tuscany. Fragments of the curtains have survived. A work table presented to the Nevilles by Queen Charlotte was also once displayed here.

Lord Braybrooke's Sitting Room Lord Braybrooke's Sitting Room was formed by throwing together the State Dressing Room and Ante Room of Lord Howard's State Apartment. The removal of the partition meant that a new ceiling and unifying frieze were required. Here was worked out the full extent of the pattern of the truncated Jacobean ceiling in the South Library. The overmantel may have been brought from the north wing, but the bright steel stove-grate of the State Dressing Room was retained.

The new room was designed to display the cream of the cabinet pictures from the three collections. A red flock wallpaper, now replaced with silk, was chosen as the background and heavy gilt fillets on the sides and along the base of the wall strengthened the very architectural effect of the picture hanging. Despite recent losses, enough of the original hanging scheme survives to convey the splendid effect of the carefully chosen and balanced subjects.

The room was intended as a drawing room, but, in practice, the Saloon was found

Lord Braybrooke's Sitting Room, photographed in 1891 by Bedford Lemere
National Monuments Record

to be adequate for this purpose, and so Lord Braybrooke annexed it for his own use. Because of the loss of later furniture the room now appears much as it was in his time. The ensemble created for Lord Howard's adjoining Saloon was preserved here,

and consists of the white-ground carpet, thought to be by Whitty of Axminster and its matching chairs, upholstered in 1786 in Thomas Moore's 'patent tapestry.' The chairs are of mahogany, but their white paint, like that on much of the other furniture in the house, is the taste of the late nineteenth century.

The inlaid walnut table in the bay may have been the centre table of the intended drawing room as it is the only piece of furniture made c1830 in the style of the new suite. Four fine pieces of French furniture possibly from the Cornwallis collection were placed in this room. Against the end walls are a pair of Boulle cabinets for the display of porcelain. In the centre of the room are two fine writing tables for Lord Braybrooke's use. On the left is a Louis XVI one in neo-classic style signed by Montigny while the other, which is unsigned, is inlaid with flowers and earlier in style. A red Boulle Louis XV clock hangs between the windows.

To complete the room in 1834, Lord Braybrooke commissioned from H W Pickersgill the portrait of Lady Jane which has place of honour among the pictures. A bust by Bacon of her grandfather, the first Marquess Cornwallis, stands below, and the japanned fire screens were painted by her mother.

The Saloon

The Saloon was last painted in 1786. It survived the changes elsewhere in the house because its decoration appealed to successive generations. Much of this appeal derives from its surviving Jacobean features. The ceiling panels, based largely on contemporary engravings, depict engaging scenes of sea monsters, merfolk and ships. The frieze and the capitals of the pilasters of the panelling have an infinite series of variations on the Howard lion crest; those in the frieze were rescued from the panelling of the Long Gallery, demolished in 1753. The panels of which they form part were 'stretched' to fit their present position by the insertion of pine slips. The consoles are also Jacobean, but the remainder of the woodwork, including the pilasters, is probably the work of Lord Howard.

When Adam replanned the house this became the Breakfast Room, conveniently sited on the bedroom floor. Breakfast was taken in the west bay after morning prayers in the Chapel. The bay has a platform raised a few steps above the floor, so that those at the table could enjoy the view.

In fitting up the room Sir John was able to find an appropriate home for his full-length family portraits which would not fit

into the low-ceilinged Great Apartments below. The size of the room enabled him to complete the full cycle of generations illustrating his descent from the original recipient of Walden Abbey, Thomas Lord Audley. The earlier pictures in the series, and those of Sir John and his mother, were painted by Rebecca. Althouth the former might be dismissed as merely imaginary, pains were taken to try to achieve authentic likenesses. The quatrefoils in the frieze were added at this time, replacing more 'sea monsters swimming.'

The newly decorated room was also the morning room. It was used until the house party changed into evening clothes and assembled in the Great Drawing Room before dinner. In contrast to the formality of the latter, it was a lighthearted room equipped with billiard tables, a harpsichord and indoor games for rainy days.

In 1784 the original purpose changed, and the room was promoted in status over the Great Apartments to form the Saloon off which opened the State Apartment. To indicate this change, the room was sumptuously gilded. At the same time the ensemble of carpet and chair covers now shown next door was introduced. At this time too Rebecca decorated the chimneypiece and added portraits of Henry VIII who gave the Abbey to Lord Audley, and Queen Elizabeth who originally granted the barony of Howard de Walden.

The result was an immensely attractive and unusually flexible room, grand enough to receive the King without being so overpowering that it was incapable of being used for other purposes. Although it lacked the absolute perfection of Adam's neo-classical Great Apartments, its blend of modern comfort and ancient splendour established a uniquely appropriate style for Audley End.

The Saloon with its 1786 furnishings replaced

In the nineteenth century the Saloon became a favourite room of the Nevilles. It may have been the second Lord Braybrooke who introduced the comfortable stuffed sofas and large Axminster carpet. Once it began to be used as an evening sitting room, the inconvenient lack of any connection between it and the Adam Dining Room must have been daily apparent. It is therefore hardly surprising that the third lord decided to form a new suite of reception rooms adjoining the Saloon and decorated to harmonise with its successful scheme.

He and Lady Jane added richer furniture. Of this only the boulle table survives at the house. It has an early top but the frame was made to match it c1820. A magnificent rosewood centre-table is partnered by a matching sofa table which was one of two. The former was displaced by the huge ottoman c1850, now a rare survival. A variety of comfortable chairs was scattered through the room. Six stuffed chairs from the same long set as those in the adjoining room were recovered in needlework by the ladies of the family. The chairs all had matching loose covers in red chintz. Two sofas from the original suite remain where they were first placed 200 years ago. The red damask curtains are those made for the third Lord Braybrooke.

Visitors now return to the Great Stair, by which the Saloon should more properly have been approached

The Park

Audley End Park, one of the finest eighteenth-century landscape gardens in England, was created by Sir John Griffin Griffin, later Lord Howard, between 1762–97, and ran for between 2 and 3 miles (3 and 5km) along the shallow valley of the River Cam. Since the Second World War large areas near the house have been returned to pasture, but many of the more distant parts have fallen into decay, and the great lake to the south of the Adam bridge has silted up. The park is thus but a shadow of its former magnificence, recorded in a series of almost photographic views by William Tomkins in the 1780s.

The outline of the design was established by 'Capability' Brown in 1762 (page 35). Brown had not only to contend with what remained of the Jacobean formal gardens, but also with two public roads that cut the park near the house—the main road from Camridge to London and a side road leading to Saffron Walden. His solution made a virtue of necessity. The barriers of the enclosed Jacobean landscape were swept away (or more frequently diguised) so that the public could enjoy the great cyclical panorama of the park focusing on the house. To provide a foreground, the Cam was dammed to make a lake. The road to Walden was given an elegant neo-classical bridge to Adam's design. To close the vista to the west, opposite the house, Adam designed the circular Temple of Victory on Ring Hill, celebrating the conclusion of the Seven Years' War. The axial Jacobean western approach to the house was replaced by informal carriage sweeps and obtrusive features such as the Jacobean red-brick stable block and the kitchen gardens were concealed by belts of planting.

The impression given to passers-by, that they were admitted to a private domain, was the result of skilful illusion. Brown also provided an entirely separate park that the family and their guests could enjoy in privacy. The outer belt of planting delimiting the 'public prospect' was in reality an inner circle of trees hiding the private part of the park, which was much larger and formed from the old deer park which lay to the north east of the house. To restrain the deer, Brown, in the second part of his plan, provided a great semi-circular ha-ha with a walk along it allowing enjoyment of the hemicycle of landscape in the direction of Saffron Walden, which was planted with oaks. This walk connected the flower garden to the south, sited beneath the windows of Adam's Drawing Rooms, with Lady Griffin's ornamental dairy, the only one of Adam's new office buildings not to be concealed by trees. To terminate the vista Sir John erected a column crowned by an urn in memory of his aunt.

Sir John quarrelled with Brown over the cost of these improvements and completed the design himself with a number of lesser advisers.

Right above: The lake and carriage road by Garvey

Below: The house from the Park by William Tomkins

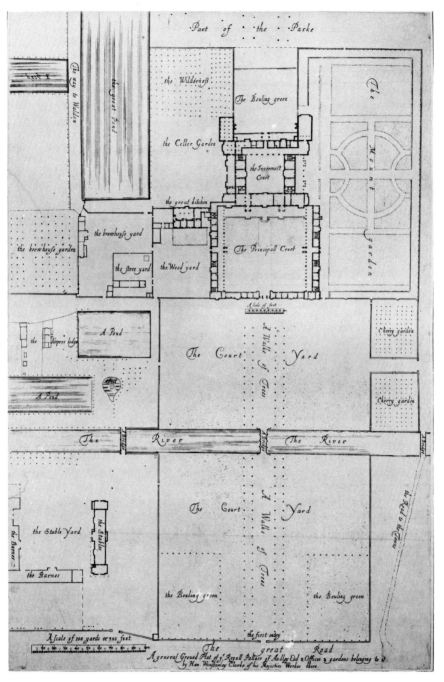

Part of the Parke

the Wilderneß

The Bouling green

the Celler Garden

the Innermost Court

the great kitchen

The way to Walden

the great Pond

The Mount Garden

the brewhouse yard

the brewhouse garden

the store yard

the Wood yard

The Principall Court

A scale of feet

Cherry garden

the Keepers lodge

A Pond

The Court Yard

A Walke of Trees

A Pond

Cherry garden

The River

The River

The Court Yard

A Walke of Trees

the Stable Yard

the Stable

the Barnes

the Barnes

the Bouling green

the Bouling green

A scale of 100 yards or 300 feet

the first entry

The great Road

A general Ground Plat of yᵉ Royall Pallace of Audley End & Offices & gardens belonging to it
by Hen. Winstanley Clarke of his Majesties Workes there.

'A General Ground Plot' *of Audley End by Henry Winstanley c1676*   Essex Record Office

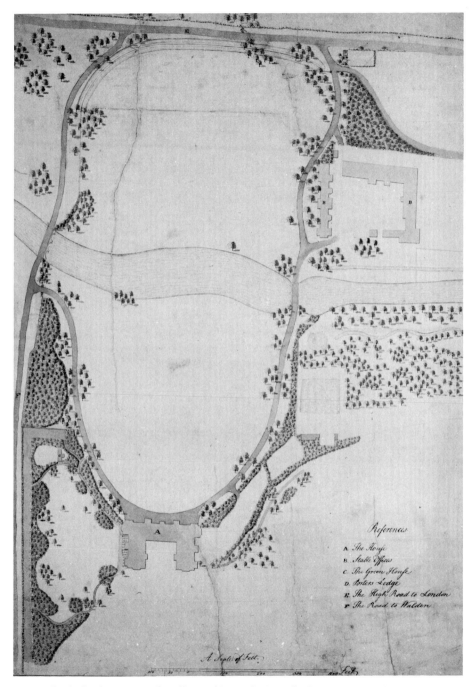

Design for the landscape west of Audley End House by Lancelot Brown

Right above: The Park in relation to the landscape of the Cam Valley

Below: The immediate environs of the house

1 *Kitchen Court,* formed *c*1762–87: A, Kitchen block; B, Laundry; C, Dairy; D, Brewhouse
2 *Flower Garden,* designed by William Gilpin, 1832
3 *Coade Stone Altar,* moved from Elysian Garden *c*1835
4 *Temple of Concord,* designed by R W F Brettingham, 1790, with Coade stone sculptures by Rossi
5 *Ice House* plantation
6 *Jacobean Gate* in park wall (blocked)
7 *South Wall of Mount Garden,* a Jacobean heightening in brick of the Tudor stone rubble wall
8 *West Wall of Mount Garden,* of Jacobean brick, with a single surviving bastion
9 *Lion Gate,* rebuilt 1786
10 *Audley End Lodge,* designed by Thomas Rickman
11 *Stone Bridge,* designed by Robert Adam, 1763; altered 1784
12 *Stable Bridge*
13 *Cambridge Lodge,* designed by Thomas Rickman, 1834
14 *Stable Block,* built *c*1605–15, much altered later
15 *Boathouse*
16 *Cascade,* designed by Richard Woods, 1783
17 *Palladian Bridge,* designed by Robert Adam, 1782
18 *Temple of Victory,* designed by Robert Adam, 1771–72
19 *Lady Portsmouth's Column*
20 *Site of Lake,* 1770; now silted
21 *London Avenue*
22 *St Mark's College,* Jacobean almshouses, now home for retired clergy
23 *Ring Hill Camp,* Iron Age hill fort
24 *Home Farm*
25 *Polish Memorial*

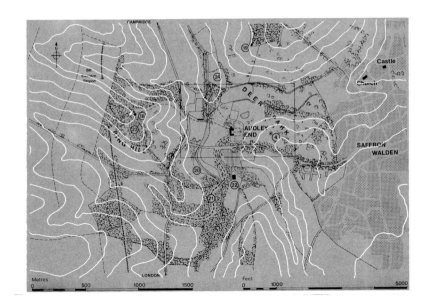

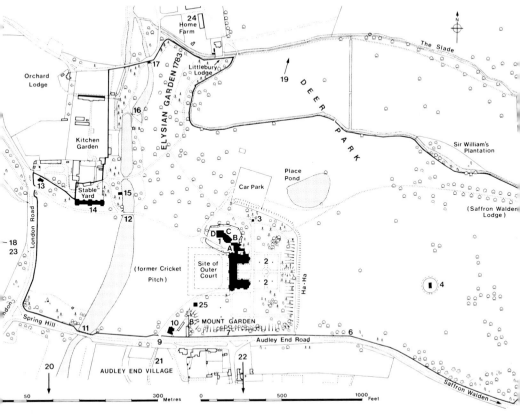

The house from the east c1875

For the pleasure of Sir John's guests the Iron Age hillfort on Ring Hill, which was approached by private drives, was provided with a menagerie of exotic birds, hidden behind the inner circle of planting and contained in a Gothick pavilion which also had a room for tea. In 1783 he formed a rival attraction nearer the house by converting the former mill lade to the north-west into an 'Elysian Garden.' The Cam was transformed into a cascade, the waters

the Corinthian 'Temple of Concord' to celebrate George III's recovery from illness. It is apparently casually placed to close the vista east of the house but can also be seen on the Walden Avenue, when the house itself is concealed from view because of its low lying position. The resulting combination of real and artificial scenery was enlivened by deer from the Duke of Beaufort's herd, a flock of Jacob's sheep and a pair of 'feluccas' or skiffs painted blue and yellow for boating on the lakes.

Later owners of the house preserved this pleasing and practical design. The third Lord Braybrooke gradually rebuilt the lodges, formerly in the guise of classical temples, in an appropriate Jacobean style to designs by Thomas Rickman. He also threw the Elysian Garden into the park, opening up the vista to Lady Portsmouth's column, because it had proved to be a frost pocket. He compensated for its loss by enlarging the flower garden east of the house into a parterre designed by William Gilpin. As well as being more practical this had the merit of recovering something of the formality of the Jacobean setting. The flower beds disappeared after the Second World War and much of its screen of shrubberies has now been removed to open up the view over the park.

In 1983, an urn was erected to the south-west of the house to commemorate the Polish members of the Special Operations Executive who trained at Audley End between 1942–44 for secret parachute missions into enemy-occupied Poland, and who perished in the service of Britain and their own country.

of which passed under a 'Palladian Bridge' which Adam designed in 1782. A circular walk dotted with flower beds inside a screen of yews led round the sheet of water. A statue of Flora, a tent and a Coade-stone altar added to its delights.

In 1792 Matthew Brettingham designed

Architectural history of Audley End to 1762

c1140–1538: Walden Abbey

Audley End stands on the site of the Bene-dictine house of St Mary and St James at Walden. It was founded as a priory c1140 by Geoffrey de Mandeville, Earl of Essex, and advanced to the status of an Abbey by Richard I in 1190. Archaeological excava-tions have shown that the inner, 'little' court of the Jacobean house, three sides of which survive to form the basis of the present house, coincides with the abbey cloister. The Jacobean walls rise from the stubs of their medieval predecessors, there being a difference in floor level of about 3ft (0.9m) between the two buildings. In the final layout of the abbey, adopted towards the close of the twelfth century, the church lay on the north side of the cloister. From the twelfth until the early fifteenth century, it was the burial place of many of the de Bohun family, Earls of Essex.

c1538–1605: the Tudor House

The convent surrendered the abbey and its possessions to Henry VIII on 22 March 1538. The whole was granted on 27 March to Sir Thomas Audley, as part of his reward as Speaker (from 1529) of the Parliament that passed the Acts for the dissolution of the monasteries. In January 1533 he had become Lord Chancellor, and in 1538 was created Baron Audley of Walden. In his will dated 1544 he described Walden Abbey or Audley 'Inn' as his 'chiefe and capital man-sion house at Walden.'

A late eighteenth-century copy of part of a now-lost estate map of c1600 (page 41) shows the first Audley End House before its Jacobean rebuilding and reveals that, probably for reasons of economy and speed, Lord Audley had converted the monastic buildings to domestic use. The north range, formerly the nave of the abbey church, dominates the others, as one would expect, and appears to have been divided into three storeys. The central tower, north transept, presbytery, Lady Chapel and other buildings were demolished and a second storey, roofed in a series of gablets, seems to have been added to the cloister walk, to give access to the first-floor rooms. The main entrance, indicated by the porch, lies at the north end of the west range, on the site of the entrance to the monastic cloister. The entrance should lead into the screens passage, indicating that the hall lay in the west range. This aspect of the layout of the house seems to anticipate that of its successor, as the hall and the entrance to the screens passage occupy the same position in the Jacobean house. Hence there was a considerable degree of structural continuity, not only between Walden Abbey and the Tudor house, but also, and perhaps more surprisingly, between them both and the Jacobean house.

The house descended via Audley's daugh-ter to Thomas Howard, fourth Duke of Norfolk, executed in 1572 for conspiring with Mary Queen of Scots. Subsequently his brother, Henry Howard, later Earl of Northampton, lived there, and supervised the education of the late duke's children. Of

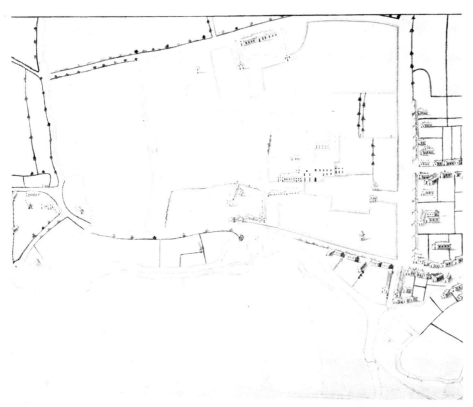

A plan of the Tudor Audley End House and Park: a late-eighteenth-century copy of a lost pre-c1605 original

these, Philip, the eldest, died in disgrace as a Catholic, but the second son, Thomas, was knighted by Elizabeth I for his gallantry in command of a ship in the fleet which defeated the Armada. He was created Baron Howard of Walden in 1597 and a Knight of the Garter in the following year.

c1605–68: the Jacobean House

After the accession of James VI of Scotland to the English throne in 1603, the fortunes of the Howard family rapidly improved. Within two months, Thomas Howard was created Earl of Suffolk and Lord Chamberlain of the Household. In 1614 he became Lord Treasurer, but was relieved of that office in July 1618, on suspicion of embezzlement. The matter came to trial in November 1619. The earl and his countess, Catherine Knevit, were found guilty and committed to the Tower; but after nine days they were released, having promised to pay a fine of £30 000, commuted in the following year to £7000. After the trial, Thomas Howard retired to Audley End, where he died in May 1626.

The downfall of the earl and countess was

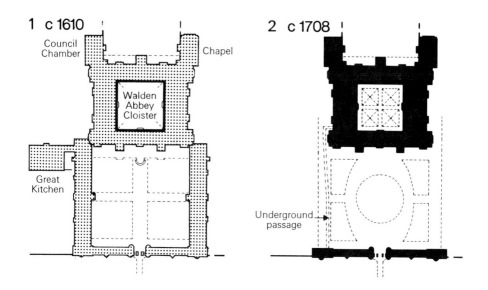

1 c 1610

Council Chamber

Chapel

Walden Abbey Cloister

Great Kitchen

2 c 1708

Underground passage

5 c 1753

Reduced to one storey

6 c 1770

0   50   100   150 metres

0   100   500 feet

3 c 1725

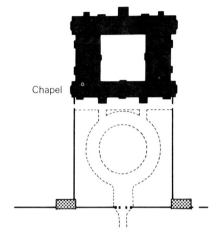

Chapel

4 c 1736

Loggia infilled

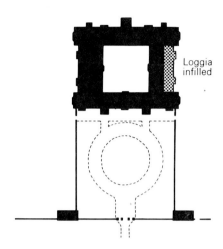

7 c 1785

Raised to three storeys

8 c 1835

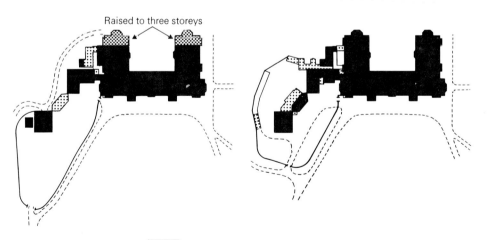

New at each phase

Exterior drastically altered

Retained from previous phase

A GENERAL PROSPE

Henry Winstanley's General Prospect of
the Royal Palace of Auydlyene, *c1676*
Essex Record Office

attributed to their rebuilding of Audley End,
their generally lavish spending, and the
rapacity of the countess. According to Philip,
Earl of Pembroke, Lord Suffolk told King
James that Audley End, including its furnishings, had cost him £200 000. This was

probably no exaggeration, but unfortunately
the building accounts do not survive; indeed
tradition has it that they were deliberately
destroyed during the progress of the work.
Casual references elsewhere, however, show
that the work took place largely between
*c*1605 and 1614.

In the absence of building accounts our
knowledge of the Jacobean house derives
substantially from the magnificent series of

engravings made, probably soon after 1676, by Henry Winstanley of Littlebury (page 46). From 1679 Winstanley was Clerk of Works for Audley End and the King's house at Newmarket, in day-to-day charge of maintenance work undertaken by the Office of Works. His survey forms probably the earliest full pictorial record of any English country house.

Recent discoveries suggest that the Jaco-bean house was built, or at least conceived, in two stages, the first comprising the four ranges round the inner court. In effect, the Tudor house was rebuilt, probably wing by wing, beginning with the west (hall) range. This phase also included the Chapel, Council Chamber, and Great Kitchen. The result was a house essentially complete in itself, and it must be this first phase which the Earl of Northampton 'assisted his *Nephew* the *Earl of Suffolk* by his designing and large contribution.' The noble patron was evidently also assisted by Bernard Janssen, a mason of Flemish descent. The extent of each man's contribution to the result is unclear. Janssen's role may have been anything between master mason and the main author of the design. The courtyard and the dominant position of the hall derive directly from the Tudor house, but following the trend set by great houses of the late sixteenth century, the important rooms and correspondingly large windows face outwards rather than into the courtyard. The designers of this first phase produced an almost elegantly simple layout, in which the disposition and relative importance of the main elements of the interior, particularly those on the first (principal) floor, were clearly, directly and harmoniously reflected in the architecture of the exterior.

The rather austere style of this first phase

Henry Winstanley's prospect of the house from the south, c1676

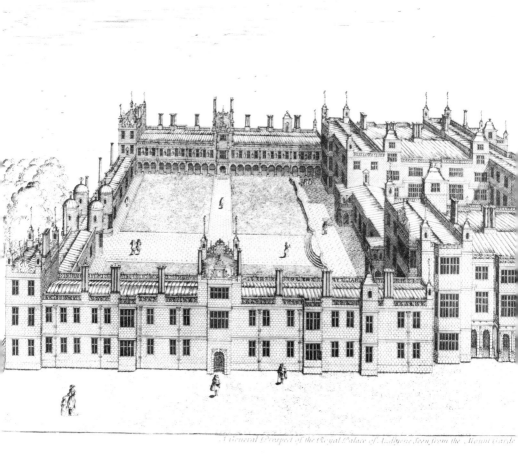

of Audley End represents the final stage in the development of Tudor, and thus perpendicular, Gothic. The large windows lack any overt Gothic details, yet here as, for example, at Hardwick Hall, through their height, size, emphasised verticals and panelled screen-like effect they convey much of the spirit of the Perpendicular style. Tradition was supplemented by Anglo-Flemish mannerist classical details and decoration, although used with restraint. Two elements of the exterior were treated differently. Decorated and Perpendicular

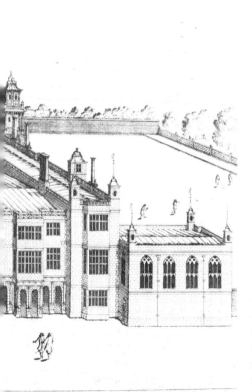

Gothic remained the architectural expression of the Anglican Church of the reigns of Charles I and James I, hence it is not surprising to find that the windows of the chapel, which projected from the south-east corner of the house, were in a style essentially of the second half of the fifteenth century. Equally, a Doric arcade was felt appropriate for the loggia on the south elevation.

The second phase in the development of the Jacobean house was the addition of the outer court. The 'book of architecture' of the Elizabethan and Jacobean surveyor, John Thorpe (now in Sir John Soane's Museum), includes a plan of Audley End, which differs substantially from Winstanley's survey of c1676 (pages 48–9). It appears to be a survey of the inner court ranges, to which is attached a scheme for the addition of an outer court, related to, but substantially different from the final design. As the style of the outer court ranges seems to accord with Thorpe's tastes, it is probable that Thorpe designed the additions. The outer ranges, now demolished, were more highly decorated than those around the inner court. The difference is illustrated by the contrast between the exuberance of the surviving porches and the simplicity of the doorcases within. That the porches belong with the second phase is demonstrated by the fact that they are clearly added to the main wall, with consequent disruption of the string courses marking each storey (page 50). The windows provide the clearest specific contrast between the details of the two phases, there being a predominant use in the outer court of 'cross' windows, each having a single mullion and transom while, in contrast, the windows in the inner court ranges rarely have less than two mullions. Moreover, the windows of the outer court were often further elaborated by being set forward

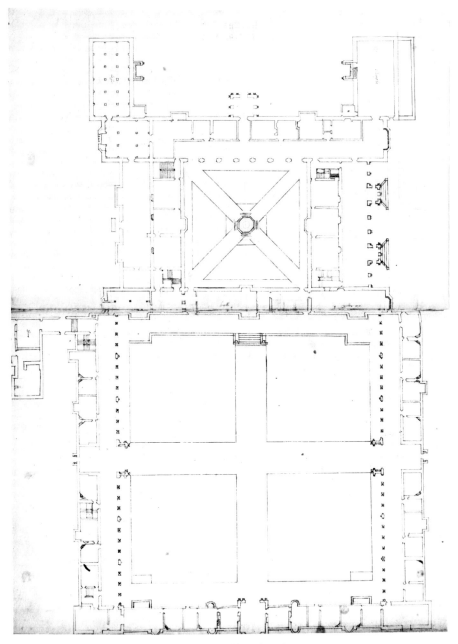

Early-seventeenth-century plan of Audley End by John Thorpe

Right: Henry Winstanley's ground plans of the outer and inner courts

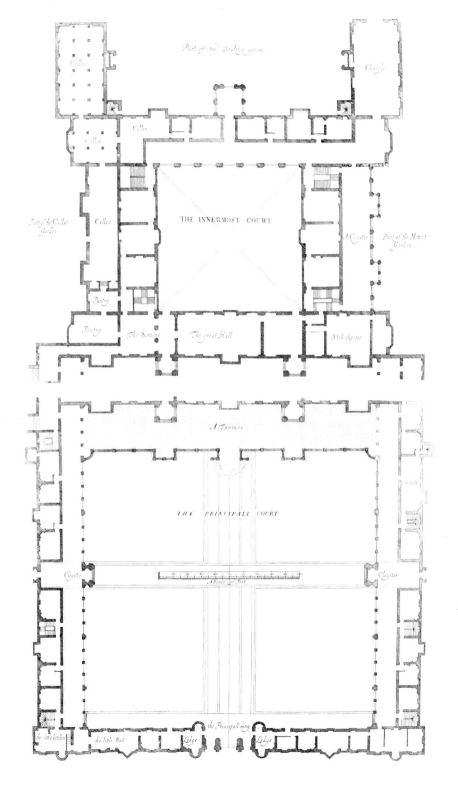

Part of the Bouling greene

Celler

Chappie

Celler

Celler

Part of the Celler Garden

Celler

THE INNERMOST COURT

A Cloyster

Part of the Mount Garden

Pantry

Pantry

The Screene

The great Hall

Still Roome

A Terrice

THE PRINCIPALL COURT

Cloyster

Scale of Feet

Cloyster

the little kitchen

the little Hall

Lodge

the Principall entry

Lodge

in projecting panels, or by having projecting sills supported on brackets, whereas those of the inner court are uniformly plain. Finally, the bay windows of the inner court ranges are all square or canted, whereas there were triangular and semi-circular ones on the west elevation of the outer court.

There is nothing distinctive or innovative about the idea of extending a house by the creation of a second courtyard. But the general form and many of the details of the outer court ranges may have been inspired by French mannerist architecture of the third quarter of the sixteenth century. This was known in early seventeenth-century England particularly through *Le premier volume des plus Excellents Bastiments de France* published in Paris by J Androuet du Cerceau in 1576 (second volume 1579). The use of four-light 'cross' windows and projecting sills supported on brackets is common in sixteenth-century French buildings, but more specifically there appears to be a correlation between Audley End and du Cerceau's engravings of the Chateau of Verneuil, begun c1565. The north and south internal elevations to the outer court at Audley End seem to be related to the design for the gallery elevation to the courtyard at Verneuil, while a design for the entrance front at Verneuil may have provided the inspiration for the entrance front at Audley End. The gatehouse itself, however, seems to owe much to the King Street gate of Whitehall Palace (1548; demolished 1723).

A third theme that runs through the design of the house is the use in a romantic or symbolic fashion of architectural features originally associated with fortifications, to express a nostalgic link with the medieval age of chivalry. Most notable is the profusion of small turrets, each with a weathervane in the form of a pennant. These belong to

The North Porch c1835; the pedestals of the lower order and the parapet date from the mid 1760s

the second phase of the Jacobean building campaign and provided a stylistic link between the two courtyards. On the entrance front, the alternate semi-circular and triangular bay-windows were repeated as mock bastions in the wall which continued the line of the elevation southwards. This retained a raised earthen terrace which offered a view over the parterres of the Mount Garden. The effect would have been that of standing on a medieval wall walk.

It seems probable that Thomas Howard at first intended to rebuild Audley End on a rather larger scale than other contemporary great houses, very much in the insular style and following the outline of the earlier house. At some point, perhaps around 1608 or 09, when this building was well advanced, his ambition seems to have grown to the point where he did not feel that it was adequate to his station and decided to add a second courtyard, perhaps more for architectural effect than for the extra accommodation it provided. The result was, in architectural terms, the nearest approach to a royal palace to be newly built in England in the first half of the seventeenth century.

Thomas Howard's house was designed to suit his particular needs and reflect his status. To suit their own needs, determined by their status, means and contemporary social custom, subsequent owners changed the uses to which rooms were put, the layout of the interior and the size of the house itself. Eighteenth- and nineteenth-century owners lacked either the means or the inclination completely to rebuild the

mansion; thus the interior as it now exists is the culmination of many successive phases of rearrangement and redecoration.

The Jacobean Audley End was, in its final form, the largest of the Elizabethan and Jacobean 'prodigy houses': that is to say, it was especially large and grand, built with the express intention of accommodating the reigning monarch in suitable style, its owner hoping to gain royal favour. Some of these houses, including Audley End, were later acquired by the Crown. Its planning was almost entirely dictated by the needs of a visiting royal household, with the State Apartments on the first floor of the inner court ranges, the family apartments on the ground floor below and lodgings for the household and servants on the second floor above or in the outer court. The relative importance of the three floors of the inner court ranges is reflected in their varying storey heights, marked externally by simplified entablatures, and emphasised by the varying heights of the windows.

West wall of the Mount Garden in 1835
Essex Record Office

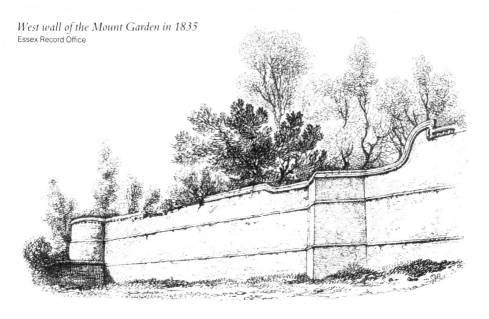

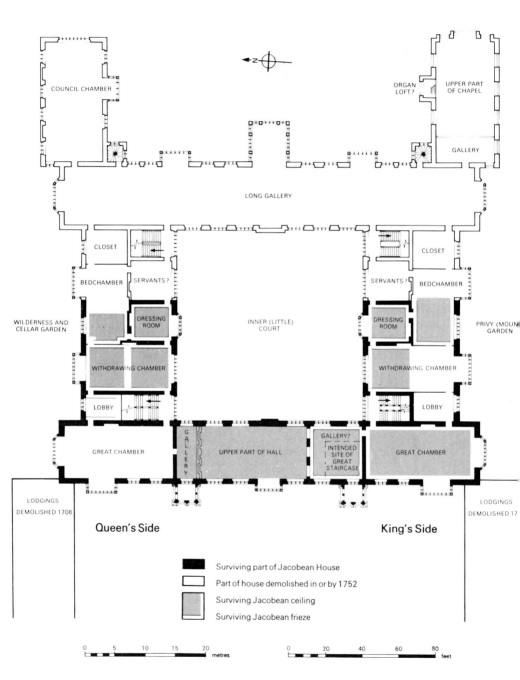

COUNCIL CHAMBER

ORGAN LOFT?

UPPER PART OF CHAPEL

GALLERY

LONG GALLERY

CLOSET

CLOSET

BEDCHAMBER

SERVANTS?

SERVANTS?

BEDCHAMBER

WILDERNESS AND CELLAR GARDEN

DRESSING ROOM

INNER (LITTLE) COURT

DRESSING ROOM

PRIVY (MOUN GARDEN

WITHDRAWING CHAMBER

WITHDRAWING CHAMBER

LOBBY

LOBBY

GREAT CHAMBER

GALLERY

UPPER PART OF HALL

GALLERY?

INTENDED SITE OF GREAT STAIRCASE

GREAT CHAMBER

LODGINGS DEMOLISHED 1708

Queen's Side

King's Side

LODGINGS DEMOLISHED 17

Surviving part of Jacobean House

Part of house demolished in or by 1752

Surviving Jacobean ceiling

Surviving Jacobean frieze

0 5 10 15 20 metres

0 20 40 60 80 feet

The layout of the north range as the King's apartment c1670
The Queen's apartment in the south range was organised similarly

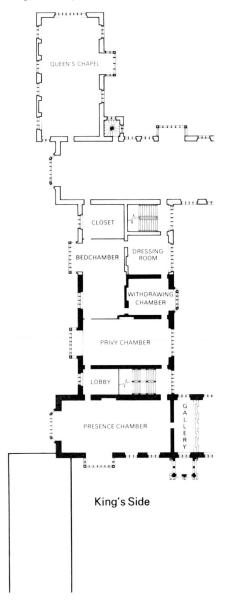

QUEEN'S CHAPEL

CLOSET

DRESSING ROOM

BEDCHAMBER

WITHDRAWING CHAMBER

PRIVY CHAMBER

LOBBY

GALLERY

PRESENCE CHAMBER

King's Side

The reconstructed first-floor plan (opposite) is based on a survey of 1752, amplified by evidence from investigation of the surviving structure, the Office of Works accounts, and the seventeenth-century ground-plans and views. As we have no direct evidence for the size of Thomas Howard's household, the regulations for its governance, or the uses to which individual rooms in the house were put, we can only interpret the plans in the light of practice in other contemporary, better-documented buildings.

Except on rare occasions, only servants would have eaten in the Great Hall (see plan, page 48), with the steward presiding at the high table on the dais. The earl would normally eat in the Parlour—at Audley End beyond the dais and the Great Staircase. To the east of the Parlour, in the north side of the south range, was an apartment of three rooms. This was probably the earl's private suite, consisting of a withdrawing room (or possibly winter parlour), bedchamber and closet. The matching suite in the south side of the north range may have been the countess's private apartment. Aristocratic marriages were essentially diplomatic alliances; such formal separation would be usual.

Royal marriages, similarly, were political alliances; such circumstances dictated not only separate apartments, but, because the Queen was entitled to respect in her own right, almost equally grand apartments. In England these were normally on the same level, and, if possible, symmetrically arranged. Hence we find at Audley End two State Apartments on the first floor, linked on the east by a Long Gallery and on the west by a hall. They were virtually identical in layout, and there was a direct route to each of them from the outer court, via the two surviving porches. The differences between them lay largely in the grandness of the approach and the degree of decoration, now reflected only in the surviving modelled plaster ceilings. The south apartment overlooked the Privy (Mount) Garden, had the finest ceilings and was intended to be approached via a great staircase opening from the south (dais) end of the hall. The north apartment overlooked the Cellar Garden and Wilderness and was approached from the screens passage by one of the four corner stairs, which although larger than the other three could not compare with the intended great staircase. Thus it is probable, but not certain, that the southern apartment was intended for the King, and the northern for the Queen. The Long Gallery, apart from linking the two apartments, gave access both to the Council Chamber and the Chapel Gallery.

Each of the State Apartments proper appears to have consisted of a Great Chamber, in which meals would have been taken on grand occasions; a lobby, leading to the Withdrawing Chamber; a Bedchamber and a Closet. All faced outwards, towards the gardens. The rooms in each range that faced wholly into the courtyard probably served as a dressing room and servants' room (giving on to the backstairs). On grand occasions when royalty was not present, Thomas Howard would probably have used one of these suites himself, or at least the Great Chamber and Withdrawing Chamber. Both suites seem to have had access to galleries overlooking the hall (from opposite ends), a reflection, no doubt, of another feature of the Great Hall, as a place in which entertainments might be performed.

The addition of the outer court produced not only further lodgings, probably only fully used during royal visits, but what was virtually a house within a house, centred on the north-west pavilion. Accommodation included a Little Hall, Little Kitchen and probably also, on the first floor, a Little Gallery and a Nursery. This complex is likely to have provided less formal accommodation for the earl and countess, and after 1668 was the lodging of the Earls of Suffolk as keepers of the palace.

The layout of the Jacobean formal gardens and the environs of the house are illustrated in slightly idealised form in Winstanley's *General Ground Plot* (page 34). Comparison between this and the plan of the environs of the Tudor house (page 41) shows how much was retained from the previous phase, a substantial part of which was itself monastic in origin. Of the Jacobean outbuildings, only the stable block survives, much rebuilt in the late seventeenth century and later. The almshouses in Audley End village (now St Mark's College) were also built by Thomas Howard in a similar style.

1668–1701: the Royal Palace

On the death of Thomas Howard in May 1626, Audley End and its builder's debts passed to his eldest son Theophilus. When he in turn died in 1640, the debts acknowledged by the third earl, James, amounted to some £55 000. During 1640–41 some £50 500 was raised by the sale of property, but the final solution to the burden created by the house and accumulated debts was provided by Charles II. 'Many ancient houses of the Crown having been demolished, we have taken a liking to Audley End'; after an inspection in March 1666, the King decided to buy it. The purchase price was £50 000, of which £20 000 was to remain on mortgage. In 1668 the Office of Works took responsibility for its maintenance.

As its original layout was effectively that of a palace, the use of Audley End as such necessitated no major alterations to the structure, as the Office of Works accounts show. But in the sixty years since its conception, the complexity of State Apartments had increased. The rooms of a State Apartment were not private in the modern sense. Various persons were allowed access to the monarch; the higher one's rank, the further one penetrated along the axis of honour, into the apartment. Not unnaturally the number of rooms in the sequence tended to increase with time. When Audley End was built, the royal lodgings contained all the rooms that one would find in the State Apartments of contemporary palaces, save for a Guard Chamber at the beginning of the sequence. By the time Charles II acquired the house as a new palace, the number of rooms along the axis of honour had increased, making it necessary to bring the former Dressing Room into the sequence, and thus incidentally to destroy the simple linear progression through the suite. The sequence, attested by the Office of Works accounts, became *Presence Chamber,* Lobby, *Privy Chamber, Withdrawing Chamber, Bedchamber* and *Closet,* the former servant's room probably becoming the Dressing Room. Moreover, since in 1668 there was only a 'great void place intended for ye great staircase,' whether because the house was never completed or because replacement was intended, the suite with the grandest approach became the northern one. From 1668, this was certainly the King's apartment, probably reversing the original intention (page 53).

The house, which the Duke of Saxe-Weimar in 1613 had thought superior to all the King's houses on account of its magnificent architecture, by the middle of the century looked distinctly old fashioned. John Evelyn in 1654 damned it with faint praise: 'It is a mixt fabric, twixt antique and modern, but observable for its being compleatly finish'd, and without comparison one of the statliest Palaces of the Kingdom.' Pepys was impressed on his first visit in 1660, but much less so seven years later, the modelled plaster ceilings by then comparing unfavourably with those of the new Clarendon House. Moreover, he thought that there was 'not one good suit of hangings in all the house, but all most ancient things, such as I would not give the hanging-up of in my house.'

Charles's initial enthusiasm for his new palace was short-lived; after 1670 neither he nor his successors made much use of it. Its maintenance, skimped by the impecunious Suffolks since its completion, was further neglected and nothing was done to modernise the interiors. Celia Fiennes in 1697 regarded them sympathetically. 'The rooms are large and lofty with good rich old furniture, tapistry, etc,' but to William III it would not stand comparison with the new work at Hampton Court or other House of Orange palaces abroad. The situation was put to the King in 1701 in the following terms:

Reasons to induce his Ma[ty] to give back Audley end house and Parke to the Rt Hon[ble] Henry Earle of Suffolke & his Children for ye Dept of £20,000 due to them.

1st That it is a place at present his Ma[ty] can make no manner of use off, the House being so very much out of Repaire, that it will cost his Ma[ty] £10,000 at least to make it habitable.

2dly That it is a Place his Ma[ty] in all likelihood will never make Use off, which appears by the Disfurnishing of it, which his Ma[ty] hath lately done.

3dly Tis not only the Dwelling house that is out of Repaire & gone to Decay, but all the Outhouses; As stables, Barnes & others are falling Downe and perishing, besides the Bridge that leads to the Stables is actually fallen into the River.

4thly The Parke wall is falling Downe in many places & the Ditches in the Parke are Choakt up with Mudd: that the currents of water which come through Walden Town are Stopt, so that part of the said Towne is over Flood.

5thly That his Ma^{ty} is at the Charge of above £600 p Ann to an Housekeeper & other Officers abt. the Repaires, which will be saved in case his Ma^{ty} disposes of it in Satisfaction of the Debt due to Earl of Suffolke & his Children which is all that they have left or their Father can give them for their Porcons.

And lastly though the Earle of Suffolke & his Children had an ample Security for the Debt of £20,000 upon the Duty arising by Chimneys [in Ireland] Yet his Ma^{ty} was pleased for the Ease of the Subject to Remitt that duty by Act of Parliament, & thereby the said Earles Security was made void.

William was glad enough to be induced: A warrant was issued for the grant on 5 August 1701.

In 1695, Sir Christopher Wren, in a letter to the Treasury, said of the building as it stood in 1668: 'the whole lead of the house was very defective, much of the timber was decay'd, and the Fabric weake, built after an ill manner rather Gay than substantiall.' It was estimated at the time of the purchase that some £10000 should be spent on repairs, 'for little had been done to it from the first foundation.' An allowance of £500 a year was made for maintainence, but this ceased with the accession of William III: from December 1688 until 1700 only about £2050 was spent.

The body of the house is of brick and the plinth and string courses of a hard Lincoln-shire limestone, but the external walls generally were faced with clunch—a form of hard chalk quarried locally. The immediate source of much of that used at Audley End was the Tudor house and ultimately Walden Abbey. The stone is very soft, and thus easily and cheaply worked; but it is also very prone to decay. Chimneystacks were particularly vulnerable; there are frequent references to repairs, and to the dismantling of disused shafts. By 1695, the stonework was in parlous state, as the then Earl of Suffolk made clear in a letter to Wren: 'Those last great windes has soe extramly shatered the chimneys of this house that it is dangerous to walke either in the Courtyard or in the Garden, great stones falling from them daily, and in that part wee lye in wee are in danger every night. There is one Great pillar in the Cloyster on the Right hand mouldered quite away at the foot of it wch if not speedily repaired the roomes in probability will tumble downe.'

So far as the use of clunch was concerned, Wren's comment was apt: a great show was made at modest expense, but with no great regard to long-term maintainence problems. Refacing has been undertaken intermittently through the eighteenth, nineteenth and twentieth centuries, largely in the rather harder Ketton stone.

'Upon the roof is a gallery, in the midst of which rises a small cupola containing a clock'; Count Magalotti's description of c1666 reflects the seventeenth century practice of taking exercise on the leads, and resorting to small banqueting rooms in the turrets. The roofs were therefore made as flat as possible, covered with thick lead to withstand the passage of feet, and edged around with stone balustrades of a convenient and safe height. To achieve a very shallow pitch, the roof joists were supported by massive oak 'camber beams,' which in places approached the limits of what was safe. Hence they distorted: some examples still in place sagged so much as to destroy the fall entirely, allowing water to penetrate the joints in the lead sheeting, which by the late seventeenth century was in any case badly cracked. Some fifty years after the original construction the roofs were clearly in a bad state. Accordingly, a rolling programme of reconstruction was set in hand, alongside general makeshift repairs. The pitches were increased (save for that of the main terrace over the Long Gallery) and the lead recast and relaid. By 1688 'half the house was new leaded, and the Roofs sub-

stantially repaired.' But the fundamental weaknesses of the structure were, and still are, such that in the absence of almost continuous maintenence the condition of the building deteriorates rapidly. This fact was significantly to influence the fate of the house during the first half of the eighteenth century.

1701–45:
Audley End House in decline

It is now clear that the house underwent three major phases of alteration between its return to the Howard family in 1701 and the death of the tenth Earl of Suffolk, the last holder of both the title and house, in 1745. During this period, no one concerned with the house had sufficient money to contemplate substantial rebuilding, indeed most were heavily in debt. Work was restric-

Audley End from the west c1710, artist unknown

ted to the demolition of subsidiary ranges, and the alteration and modernisation of the interior of the main house. The latter was probably financed largely out of the sale of materials, especially lead, from the former.

The conveyance of the house from William III was to trustees, on behalf of the five co-heirs of James, third Earl of Suffolk, in accordance with the distribution of assets in the latter's will. Although Henry, Lord Bindon, eldest son of the fifth earl, bought the shares of the other co-heirs in 1702, a legal dispute prevented his becoming uncontested owner until March 1708. Within the year, he was 'busy to the Utmost of his force in New Moulding Audley End,' with John Vanbrugh, a distant relative, as his architect. By 1713, the house was 'now most of it pulled down, there remaining only one large court, which however makes a Noble Palace to the present earl that resides there. . . .' The manner of its reduction is illustrated by an early eighteenth-century painting (page 57). This shows that the buildings evidently in the worst condition and least useful in a private house—the north and south ranges of the outer court and the great kitchen—were demolished, leaving intact the western range of the outer court and the walls extending its west elevation north and south. (See page 42.)

The prospect confronting visitors passing through the Jacobean main gate from the Cambridge road then resembled a curtain wall with gatehouse, towers, and bastions, above and beyond which the turreted bulk of the main house loomed like a medieval keep. By this separation into two blocks, and the removal of the most overtly classical

Left: Survey of Audley End Gardens and
Park after the reduction of the house c1725

elements (other than the loggia) the demolitions undoubtedly enhanced the romantic 'castle air' of the place. What had been the Little Kitchen in the north pavilion of the west range of the outer court seems to have formed the basis of the post-1708 main kitchen, for it is otherwise hard to imagine why an underground passage, part of which still survives (as the coal cellar) should have been constructed to link it to the service rooms at the north-west corner of the main house.

Lord Bindon became sixth earl in 1709, on the death of his father, and lived on at Audley End until 1718. The house then descended to his son Charles William, the seventh earl. He settled Audley End on himself and his uncle Charles, third son of the fifth earl, rather than Edward, the second son. Thus when Charles William died in 1722, Edward became eighth Earl of Suffolk, but his brother Charles inherited the property. Edward contested the settlement, with the result that in 1724, after the estate had been for a time sequestered, Charles agreed that Edward should have an annuity of £1200 a year. Charles now had more or less undisputed possession, and seems almost at once to have begun to alter the house, the work involving demolition in 1724 or 25. A chance reference in 1726 suggests that Nicholas Dubois was the architect responsible. He was of French birth, probably a Huguenot refugee, and later an officer in the British army.

A surviving plan shows the house without the original chapel or the council chamber, and with the western range of the outer court demolished save for the ground floors of the pavilions, retained as lodges at the corners of a walled and railed forecourt. The house and forecourt were intended to be the focus of a vast and grandiose formal garden on French lines, but in the event, only the changes to the house and forecourt were executed, as the survey plan of the park and gardens shows (page 58). A new two-storey chapel, entered from the vestibule, was formed in the original northern great chamber and ground-floor rooms below.

Charles Howard became ninth earl in 1731, on the death of his brother Edward without issue; he himself died in 1733, leaving the house and his debts to his son Henry, the tenth earl. Two years later, Henry achieved solvency by marrying Sarah Inwen, the daughter of a wealthy brewer. Of the £25 000 she brought with her, £18 000 was used to discharge mortgages, and some at least of the balance used to modernise the interior of the house; work was in progress by 1736. The most drastic change was the infilling of the loggia to form three extra rooms; according to the third Lord Braybrooke, writing a century later, this was done about 1740, because the earl, 'suffering from the gout, preferred to live on the ground floor.' The tenth earl also replanned the first floor, creating four new bedroom apartments from each of the Jacobean state suites.

1745–62:
Elizabeth Countess of Portsmouth

The tenth earl died in 1745, intestate and without issue. His title passed to his heir the Earl of Berkshire, and the titles subsequently descended together. However, Thomas, second Earl of Effingham, took possession of the estate on the strength of a settlement made by the seventh earl in 1721. His right to do so was contested at law, and the settlement shown to be invalid, as the seventh earl was a mere tenant for life under an earlier settlement made by James, third

Earl of Suffolk, in 1687. The estate therefore passed to the heirs of James, being divided equally between Lord Hervey, later Earl of Bristol, on the one hand, and the Countess of Portsmouth and her sister, Mrs Anne Whitwell, on the other. The only exception was Audley End House and Park, which, being Crown property in 1687, were unaffected by the third earl's actions, and passed to the Earl of Effingham under the 1721 settlement. Lady Portsmouth's share of the estate adjoined Audley End; in 1751 she purchased the house and park from Lord Effingham for £10 000.

Lady Portsmouth, who acquired her title by her second marriage, was childless, and her chosen heir was her sister's eldest son John Griffin Whitwell. Since he was contemplating settling down and was house hunting—a matter which became more pressing on his marriage in 1748 to Anna Maria Shutz—his aunt decided that he could have no more suitable home than that of his Suffolk ancestors. She therefore employed John Phillips and George Shakespear in 1752 to adapt the Suffolks' house to the more modest needs of her nephew. This they achieved by demolishing the east (Gallery) side of the court and retaining the hall as the nucleus for the smaller house. By so doing they managed to devise a house in keeping with contemporary great house plans. The Great Hall and Great Stair led to the Saloon on the first floor, off which lay the best bedroom apartment. The other first-floor rooms were converted to three lesser bedroom apartments. Below the Saloon and best bedroom were the Dining Parlour and other reception rooms. Chapel and Kitchen were retained on the north side of the hall. New eastern outer walls were carried up to close the truncated ends of the north and south ranges, and to terminate

Elevation of the East Front of Audley End, 1762

them neatly, single storey pavilions were formed at the foot of the new walls. That on the south accommodated a library and that on the north additional service space near the Kitchen.

The Gallery range was carefully dismantled and the sale of its materials helped to defray the cost of repairs. The same source also supplied the materials for the new work. Carved stonework was dismantled and reset, panelling was used in new positions and severed Jacobean friezes and ceilings carefully repaired. Althouth antiquarian critics imputed the countess's action to meanness, there can be no doubt that she worked in the Jacobean style from choice, motivated by pride in her Howard ancestry. In August 1753, in a letter to the countess, Phillips explained his design for the pavilions, adding that 'it could not be done other ways than it is, to preserve the line of Building, which is certainly the beauty of it, and it now appears the same as tho' this was part of the original Pile, which your Ladyship gave me express command to observe.'

The last vestiges of the Suffolk's furnishings had been dispersed at auction in 1745. In their place the countess introduced substantial mahogany furniture. These pieces, with her pictures, plate and books, were left to her nephew and form the basis of the present collection.

Audley End and its owners:
1762 to the present day

1762–84: Sir John Griffin Griffin

Lady Portsmouth imposed one condition on her generosity: that her nephew must change his name and arms to that of Griffin. Sir John Griffin Griffin, as he thus became, had been retired from active military service on account of the wound he received at the battle of Campen while on active service in Germany. After a distinguished career, George II honoured him with the Order of the Bath. He was elected Member of Parliament for Andover and turned his attention to improving his estates and the wider affairs of Essex.

The new owner of Audley End was forty-three when he succeeded. He was not only interested in the arts, but attuned to the world of metropolitan fashion. Within a few months of his aunt's death, he summoned both Robert Adam and Lancelot 'Capability' Brown to Audley End. They represented the most advanced taste in architecture and landscape gardening of the day and were asked to collaborate in a thorough replanning of house and park. Sir John was not as rich as many of his contemporaries, nor was he a particularly easy patron to deal with as he took an active part in all the aesthetic decisions, but the financial restraints and discerning patronage kept Adam and Brown on their mettle. Although Adam's most notable achievement was a suite of reception rooms for fashionable entertaining, his brief extended to the whole house, including the building of a new kitchen wing (detached from the house in

case of fire) and a comprehensive reconsideration of the countess's awkward planning.

In 1764 a shadow was cast by the death of his wife, Anna Maria, but the following year Sir John married Katherine Clayton, then only eighteen. The new Lady Griffin came to Audley End in time to supervise the fitting up of the interiors. Under her direction the reception rooms (completed in 1771) took on a perfection and precision which reflected her fastidious taste. By the 1770s Audley End, which had come so near to destruction just a few years before, was reinstated as one of the finest houses in the county.

1784–97: Lord Howard de Walden

In 1784 Sir John achieved his lifelong ambition when the King recognised his claim to the barony of Howard de Walden, the title granted by Queen Elizabeth to Thomas Howard. To suit Audley End for its new role as a nobleman's seat rather than a gentleman's residence, Lord Howard began a further series of alterations. The principal change was the creation of a State Apartment, sumptuously appointed for the reception of the King, from the former best bedroom apartment in the south wing. This was approached from the Saloon and reinstated the original processional route from the Great Hall up the Great Stair. To provide more accommodation for this State Apartment Lord Howard raised the single-storey pavilions on the east front to roof height, a change that greatly improved the internal plan, as it provided an interior lady's dressing room for each of the bedroom apartments on the first floor, new staircases and mezzanine service rooms in the bays, and four good rooms on the top floor.

Although Lord Howard sought advice from James Essex of Cambridge on the structural aspects of these changes, his approach was very different from that of the 1760s. By the 1780s Lord Howard was an experienced amateur architect and his wife an accomplished decorator, with sufficient confidence in their own taste to plan these changes themselves. They had also formed a skilled team of estate craftsmen under the direction of William Ivory, capable of carrying out much of the work.

The changes were rapidly completed during the summer of 1786, when the remote possibility of receiving the King became an apparent certainty. After the success of the royal visit to Oxford University when the

The house from the east in 1783 by Robinson (from Lord Braybrooke's History of Audley End)

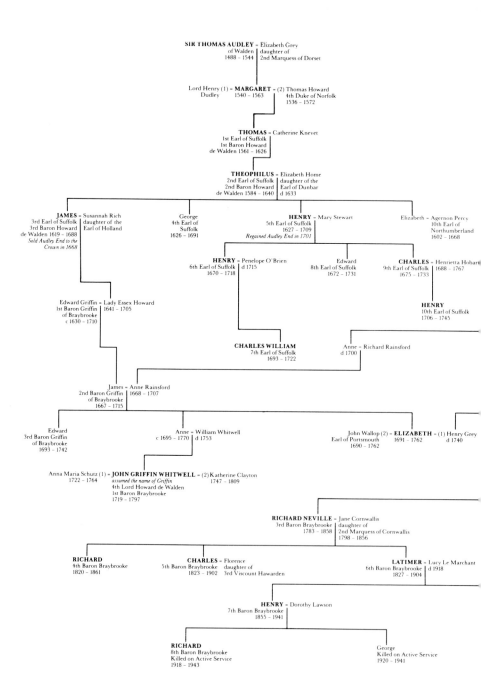

SIR THOMAS AUDLEY = Elizabeth Grey
of Walden | daughter of
1488 – 1544 | 2nd Marquess of Dorset

Lord Henry (1) = **MARGARET** = (2) Thomas Howard
Dudley | 1540 – 1563 | 4th Duke of Norfolk
1536 – 1572

THOMAS = Catherine Knevet
1st Earl of Suffolk
1st Baron Howard
de Walden 1561 – 1626

THEOPHILUS = Elizabeth Home
2nd Earl of Suffolk | daughter of the
2nd Baron Howard | Earl of Dunbar
de Walden 1584 – 1640 | d 1633

JAMES = Susannah Rich
3rd Earl of Suffolk | daughter of the
3rd Baron Howard | Earl of Holland
de Walden 1619 – 1688
Sold Audley End to the Crown in 1668

George
4th Earl of
Suffolk
1626 – 1691

HENRY = Mary Stewart
5th Earl of Suffolk
1627 – 1709
Regained Audley End in 1701

Elizabeth = Agernon Percy
10th Earl of
Northumberland
1602 – 1668

HENRY = Penelope O'Brien
6th Earl of Suffolk | d 1715
1670 – 1718

Edward
8th Earl of Suffolk
1672 – 1731

CHARLES = Henrietta Hobart
9th Earl of Suffolk | 1688 – 1767
1675 – 1733

Edward Griffin = Lady Essex Howard
1st Baron Griffin | 1641 – 1705
of Braybrooke
c 1630 – 1710

HENRY
10th Earl of Suffolk
1706 – 1745

CHARLES WILLIAM
7th Earl of Suffolk
1693 – 1722

Anne = Richard Rainsford
d 1700

James = Anne Rainsford
2nd Baron Griffin | 1668 – 1707
of Braybrooke
1667 – 1715

Edward
3rd Baron Griffin
of Braybrooke
1693 – 1742

Anne = William Whitwell
c 1695 – 1770 | d 1753

John Wallop (2) = **ELIZABETH** = (1) Henry Grey
Earl of Portsmouth | 1691 – 1762 | d 1740
1690 – 1762

Anna Maria Schutz (1) = **JOHN GRIFFIN WHITWELL** = (2) Katherine Clayton
1722 – 1764 | *assumed the name of Griffin* | 1747 – 1809
4th Lord Howard de Walden
1st Baron Braybrooke
1719 – 1797

RICHARD NEVILLE = Jane Cornwallis
3rd Baron Braybrooke | daughter of
1783 – 1858 | 2nd Marquess of Cornwallis
1798 – 1856

RICHARD
4th Baron Braybrooke
1820 – 1861

CHARLES = Florence
5th Baron Braybrooke = daughter of
1823 – 1902 | 3rd Viscount Hawarden

LATIMER = Lucy Le Marchant
6th Baron Braybrooke | d 1918
1827 – 1904

HENRY = Dorothy Lawson
7th Baron Braybrooke
1855 – 1941

RICHARD
8th Baron Braybrooke
Killed on Active Service
1918 – 1943

George
Killed on Active Service
1920 – 1941

Audley End Family Tree

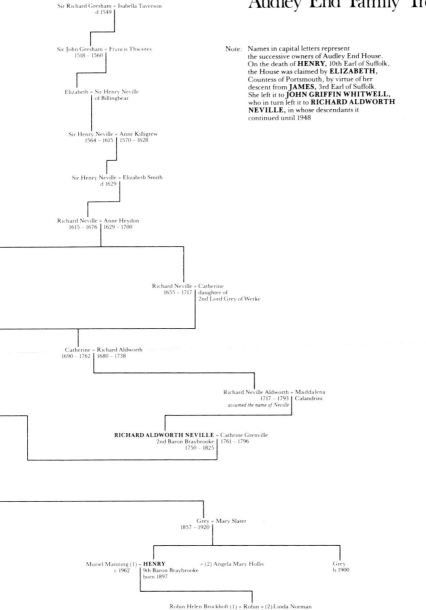

Note: Names in capital letters represent
the successive owners of Audley End House.
On the death of **HENRY**, 10th Earl of Suffolk,
the House was claimed by **ELIZABETH,**
Countess of Portsmouth, by virtue of her
descent from **JAMES,** 3rd Earl of Suffolk.
She left it to **JOHN GRIFFIN WHITWELL,**
who in turn left it to **RICHARD ALDWORTH
NEVILLE,** in whose descendants it
continued until 1948

Sir Richard Gresham = Isabella Taverson
d 1549

Sir John Gresham = Francis Thwaites
1518 – 1560

Elizabeth = Sir Henry Neville
of Billingbear

Sir Henry Neville = Anne Killigrew
1564 – 1615 | 1570 – 1628

Sir Henry Neville = Elizabeth Smith
d 1629

Richard Neville = Anne Heydon
1615 – 1676 | 1629 – 1700

Richard Neville = Catherine
1655 – 1717 | daughter of
2nd Lord Grey of Werke

Catherine = Richard Aldworth
1690 – 1762 | 1680 – 1738

Richard Neville Aldworth = Maddalena
1717 – 1793 | Calandrini
assumed the name of Neville

RICHARD ALDWORTH NEVILLE = Cathrine Grenville
2nd Baron Braybrooke | 1761 – 1796
1750 – 1825

Grey = Mary Slater
1857 – 1920

Muriel Manning (1) = **HENRY**   = (2) Angela Mary Hollis   Grey
c 1962 | 9th Baron Braybrooke   b 1900
born 1897

Robin Helen Brockhoft (1) = Robin = (2) Linda Norman
b 1932

Henrietta   Arabella   Victoria   Caroline   Amanda   Sarah   Emma
d 1980   — *Twins* —

royal party stayed at Nuneham Courtenay, the seat of Lord Harcourt, it was intimated that Cambridge would be similarly honoured and that the royal family would use Audley End as their base for the visit. Although this visit never took place because of the King's illness, the summer of 1786 was a period of intense activity at Audley End.

In 1788, Lord Howard was created the first Baron Braybrooke. Until his death in 1797 improvements continued in the park, and the collections were augmented by new furnishings, pictures and the latest books, as this childless couple channelled their energies into their house. However Lord Howard arranged that on his death his heir, Richard Neville, second Lord Braybrooke, a descendent of Lady Portsmouth's first husband, should take immediate possession of Audley End. His successor was reluctant to move, as it would necessitate Lady Howard's taking leave of her beloved home, but she concurred with her late husband's wishes and wrote to Lord Braybrooke 'Indeed I do fear I should be very unequal to it alone in any season for tho' it has afforded me indescribable happiness for 32 years its principle charm is gone. . . . The best return you can make me is living in this place with comfort to yourself and affectionate recollection of those who have inhabited it with so much delight for such a number of years.'

1797–1825:
the second Lord Braybrooke

Although Lord Howard owned land outside Essex, Audley End was his only seat. When the second Lord Braybrooke succeeded, he already possessed the Neville estates in Berkshire and was settled at Billingbear, which he had altered to suit his tastes. As

a young man he was often summoned to Audley End, so that the Howards could get to know their prospective heir, but he found the magnificence of their daily life ill-suited to his quieter temperament. His wife Catherine, sister of the Marquess of Buckingham, died in 1796, so that it was as a widower that he came with his seven children to Audley End.

He inherited a house in perfect order, and with characteristic tact refrained from any changes inside the house until after Lady Howard's death in 1809. The rebuilding of the Saffron Walden Lodge in castellated style is typical of his improvements. He also purchased additional property to consolidate the estate, such as the land of Ring Hill, west of the house, which Lord Howard had merely rented from the Earl of Bristol to carry out his landscape designs.

Within the house his alterations were minor and dictated by practical concerns. He may have had larger cases made for the Library to hold his books in addition to Lord Howard's. The North Parlours were papered to make informal sitting rooms and their pictures hung in the Gallery. He also altered Adam's Dining Parlour, to bring it into line with the fashionable requirements of his day.

In 1819 the royal visit against which Lord and Lady Howard had made such careful preparations took place. The Duke of Gloucester and his Duchess, the Princess Mary, accompanied by his sister Princess Sophia, stayed at Audley End for a few days on their way back from Cambridge. Although the etiquette was much simpler than it would have been in the 1780s, the visit was conducted with great splendour. The house was filled to capacity and thirty-seven people sat down to dinner in the new Dining Parlour.

In the same year his eldest son Richard married Lady Jane Cornwallis, and Lord Braybrooke seems to have decided to give them Audley End while he returned to Billingbear, where he died in 1825.

1825–58: the third Lord Braybrooke

Between 1825 and 1835 the third Lord Braybrooke and Lady Jane carried out a series of alterations that were almost as extensive as those of Lord Howard. Because of the chances of the pattern of inheritance that followed them, it is their taste that is stamped on the house, which today remains arranged and decorated much as they left it.

There were many reasons for these changes, from essential running repairs and the purely practical provision of nurseries for their eight children in a house which Lord Howard had arranged for adults, to wider considerations of fashion and propriety. Although Lord Howard was deeply interested in his ancestors and was an avid collector of Howard portraits, he combined these interests with the promotion of the arts of his own time. The scholarly Nevilles were better equipped to pursue the architectural history of their new seat. In 1809 the second lord had assembled a large scrapbook in which he arranged chronologically portraits of the owners of the house and topographical views and designs illustrating the changes the house had undergone. His eldest son continued to follow this interest and in 1822, while recuperating from an illness, began to study the history of the house. As he discovered more about the magnificence of the Suffolk's palace, he realised the outstanding place Audley End occupied in the history of English architecture; in 1836 his work culminated in the publication of *The History of Audley End*

and *Saffron Walden*. Although reserved about his own alterations, he unhesitatingly condemned Lord Howard's approach. The latter's Georgian Gothick chapel was particularly offensive to the archaeological taste of the new possessor: 'In the style called after its patron Strawberry Hill Gothic, a mode of decoration sufficiently objectionable under any circumstances, but perhaps never adopted with less judgement or worse effect than in a building of the date and character of Audley End.' The remainder of mid-Georgian taste was dismissed as a time 'when the arts were at a very low ebb.'

Lord Braybrooke employed the architect Henry Harrison to help him purge the house of its neo-classical decorations and re-stress its Jacobean character. But the ambitious schemes they first considered were modified in execution, to the extent that Audley End missed becoming a great antiquarian house and even the Chapel survived. The reason it escaped such a single-minded treatment was because Lord and Lady Braybrooke's architectural ambitions were rapidly submerged in the more passive role of museum curators.

While planning his improvements Lord Braybrooke had taken a decision to make Audley End his principal seat, as it was the more important house. As Audley End was now to be the seat of the Nevilles he decided to remove the principal treasures and relics from their former seat at Billingbear and incorporate them in his new arrangement. These included portraits, furniture, pictures and a library. In the same way his wife, as the eldest of the Marquess Cornwallis's daughters, who were his co-heiresses, brought to Audley End on her marriage the largest and historically the most important portion of the Cornwallis possessions which had been divided after her father's death.

Design for the interior of the Great Hall by Henry Shaw c1825

Her share included a complete picture gallery from Brome Hall in Suffolk, with a run of ancestral portraits from Tudor times, the cream of their library, plate, furniture and family relics. These included many of her grandfather, the great First Marquess Cornwallis, hero of the Indian wars and veteran of the American War of Independence.

This tidal wave of inherited possessions, in combination with the available space, eventually settled into the only suitable positions. Thus the Jacobean revival interiors they had planned, and their half-hearted attempts to collect genuine ancient furniture, to which end they visited Holland in 1828, were gradually abandoned in favour of a compromise. To help with the new decorations, which carefully copied original Jacobean decoration surviving at the house, Lord Braybrooke employed Henry Shaw, the antiquary. Artist friends, whose visits are recorded in the visitors book, were also pressed into an informal 'committee of taste' for advice.

To keep abreast of the latest ideas in domestic comfort, Lord and Lady Braybrooke set out on a series of country house tours which are recorded in Lady Jane's diaries. During these visits, the King's architect took them across scaffolding on a tour of George IV's Windsor Castle, and they visited the Grange, then the most advanced house of its day. Lady Jane particularly admired suites of interconnecting rooms, splendidly decorated and similarly hung with fine pictures, which she saw in

AUDLEY END AND ITS OWNERS

houses such as Panshanger. They reproduced this arrangement at Audley End by forming a suite of new reception rooms from Lord Howard's State Bedroom and second best bedroom apartments on the original *piano nobile* adjoining the Saloon. The new rooms had sufficient height to take the finest of the several hundred pictures that were now at Audley End, and which more than anything else had necessitated the change. The displaced bedroom suites were moved to the former reception rooms on the floor below (see the illustrations on pages 9 and 71).

These internal changes were complemented by changes in the park and to the house itself. But just as the ambitious schemes were modified inside, a proposal to build a new set of offices, recapturing something of the splendid Jacobean offices, remained on paper. An easily noticeable change was the replacement of the lead covering of the turret roofs with copper.

The third Lord Braybrooke and Lady Jane lived happily at Audley End for twenty

The Great Hall and Stair

years after their alterations were completed. Lord Braybrooke produced a number of distinguished historical works, and won fame through the singular honour he enjoyed of producing the first edition of Pepy's diaries. This he owed to the family's close connection with Magdalene College, Cambridge—Lord Braybrooke was its hereditary visitor. His other enthusiasm was cricket, and the west lawn was laid out as a pitch for which the Saloon provided a perfect grandstand for the ladies.

Lady Jane died in 1856 and Lord Braybrooke in 1858. A few years previously their third and fifth sons had been killed in the Crimean War.

1858–1904: the fourth, fifth and sixth Lords Braybrooke

Between 1858 and 1904 the third Lord Braybrooke and Lady Jane's three surviving sons succeeded to the estate as fourth, fifth and sixth Lords Braybrooke. Richard, the fourth lord, was a noted archaeologist and established a museum at the house, as well as a large collection of mounted birds. He and his wife, Lady Charlotte, had two daughters, so that on his death in 1861 he was succeeded by his brother Charles.

Major repairs to the house were carried out by the fifth lord, under the supervision of his architect Richard Hussey, who in 1863 also formed the Lower Gallery by glazing in the open portico on the east front. The fifth lord's wife, Florence, preserved Lady Jane's arrangement of the rooms, but made some minor alterations to reflect current taste. She rescued the surviving Georgian furniture made for Lord Howard, which her mother-in-law had banished to the attic. These pieces were repaired, french polished, and reupholstered for display in the main rooms. The effect was to produce rooms

of great liveliness, with a diversity of interesting contents.

The fifth lord was survived on his death in 1902 by his only daughter Augusta. His brother Latimer therefore succeeded as sixth lord. He was too old to want to settle in the house, and so Audley End was let. The tenant was, appropriately, Lord Howard de Walden, who was attracted, as Charles II had been before him, by its proximity to Newmarket. During his occupation the house enjoyed an Edwardian swansong in the great age of country house entertaining. Since the lease was short, its interiors were preserved from modernisation.

1904–48: the seventh and eighth Lords Braybrooke and the Second World War

The sixth lord died in 1904 and was succeeded by his eldest son Henry, the seventh baron, who in 1917 married as his second wife Dorothy Lawson. They had to wait until the lease expired before they could take possession of their new home. In 1916, in an act of retrenchment, Billingbear, the original home of the Nevilles, had been sold and its remaining contents were brought to Audley End, adding a further layer to its richly furnished rooms.

The seventh lord and his wife had two sons and a daughter, Catherine, and carefully preserved the house and its historic contents until the outbreak of the Second World War, when it was requisitioned. The years that followed brought personal tragedy to the Braybrooke family. Lord Braybrooke died in 1941 and a few months later his younger son was killed on active service. His elder son succeeded as eighth Lord Braybrooke but was himself killed in action in 1943 with the Grenadier Guards.

Mid-nineteenth-century watercolour of the Great Drawing Room, fitted up as the State Bedchamber by the third Lord Braybrooke c1825 (see the plan on page 9)

The house was requisitioned, not by the War Department, but by the Ministry of Works which made special arrangements to safeguard the house and its contents, all the furniture being stacked in the state rooms and Chapel, where it remained until 1945. Between May 1942 and December 1944, Audley End served as the training headquarters of the Polish section of the Special Operations Executive where volunteers were trained for clandestine operations behind enemy lines; remains of the concrete fortifications which protected them survive in the grounds today. The present Lord Braybrooke records that when he had cause to visit the Muniment Room at Audley End at the time of his inheritance in 1943 to obtain the Deed Patent of the Family Peerage and other documents he found access by no

means easy, and recalls with some amusement that the only time he was required to show his Identity Card throughout the war was when he was trying to get into his own house.

Audley End was derequisitioned in 1945 and it then became the responsibility of the Ministry of Works to restore the house to its condition at the time of requisitioning. This entailed unstacking all the furniture and replacing each piece in its proper room, an enormously difficult task in spite of the inventories that had been made. The future of the house had then to be resolved, as the Braybrooke family had already decided that as a home it was too big for them. The solution was found in 1948 when the present Lord Braybrooke sold the house to the Ministry of Works, at the same time agreeing

The west front as it is now

to lend the pictures and furniture to the Ministry free for a period of twenty-one years, on the understanding that they would take responsibility for insurance and maintenance during that period. It was an essential part of the agreement that the house was to be opened to the public at least during the summer months. Thus the house with about 100 acres (40ha) of parkland and 12 acres (5ha) of kitchen garden passed into the ownership of the nation.

Audley End today

Today Audley End is looked after by the Historic Buildings and Monuments Commission. The Braybrooke family still live on the estate, which they farm, thus preserving their link with Audley End. When the loan of the furnishings expired in 1969 the more important items were purchased for preservation with the house and in 1980 part of the contents of the family's private rooms was also purchased. Thus most of the contents remain in the positions selected for them by the third Lord Braybrooke and Lady Jane in the 1820s, and the whole is still a remarkably complete survival from the early nineteenth century. Much of the furniture and many of the pictures, however, remain the property of Lord Braybrooke's son, the Honourable Robin Neville, thanks to whose kindness they are displayed.

Glossary

ABACUS	Flat slab on top of a capital
APPLIQUÉ	Decorative technique involving the application of pieces of one fabric to the surface of another
ARMOIRE	Cupboard, usually of monumental form with pilasters, etc
BASTION	Projection from outer wall of fortification
BAS RELIEF	Decorative sculpture in low relief
BLUE JOHN	From French *bleu-jaune,* blue-yellow. Crystalline mineral mined in Derbyshire, used in making ornaments
BOLECTION MOULDING	Heavily projecting moulding used to mask joint between two members with different surface levels
BOMBÉ	Literally 'blown out'—an exaggerated shape, convex on two or more axes
BOULLE	Brass and tortoiseshell marquetry (qv), named after its most notable exponent A C Boulle (1642–1732)
CASTELLATED	Having battlements for defence or decoration
COADE STONE	Artificial cast stone manufactured by Mrs Eleanor Coade in London in the late eighteenth and early nineteenth centuries
COMMODE	Chest of drawers; used in English of decorative examples in the French style
CORINTHIAN	One of the three main orders in classical architecture, the capitals consisting largely of acanthus foliage and volutes supporting the abacus (qv)
CORNICE	Upper member of a classical entablature (qv); may be used alone at junction of wall and ceiling
CUPOLA	Small dome, often crowning a turret
DADO	Lower part of an internal wall, from the floor to a moulding at waist height.
DORIC	One of the three main orders in classical architecture, the capitals consisting only of mouldings
ENTABLATURE	In classical architecture, a horizontal assembly of architrave, frieze (qv), and cornice (qv), either supported by columns or pilasters (when the order is expressed) or used alone at the top of a wall or storey (when the order is implied)
FESTOON CURTAIN	Curtain opening and closing vertically, looped in festoons when raised
FESTOON	Ornament in the form of a garland suspended between two points

FILLET	Narrow, flat, often raised band
FRET	Geometrical pattern of continuous ornament
FRIEZE	Central part of a classical entablature (qv); less precisely, a horizontal band of ornament
GOTHICK	Light decorative style derived in the eighteenth century from medieval Gothic forms
GRISAILLE	Decorative painting in shades of grey, to give the effect of modelling in relief
GROTESQUE	Fanciful ornamental decoration, derived from Roman wall paintings, and consisting of medallions, candleabra, human and animal figures, foliage, strapwork, etc
HA–HA	Wall or fence erected in a dip or ditch so as to keep animals out of a garden or park without obstructing the view
HAMMER BEAM	Bracket projecting horizontally from top of wall to support other roof timbers
JACOBEAN	Of the reign of James I (1603–25)
JAPANNING	Imitation of oriental lacquer, usually black, dark green or red
JIB	Concealed door
KEEP	Principal tower of a castle
LOGGIA	Gallery with at least one open side, generally in the form of a classical arcade
MANNERISM	Deliberate misuse of elements of a style for architectural effect; applied thus to much western European classical architecture of the sixteenth and seventeenth centuries
MARQUETRY	Decorative veneer composed of shaped pieces of wood or other material
MERFOLK	Imaginary creatures of the sea, part human, part fish; mermaids, mermen
MEZZANINE	Floor intermediate between two principal stories
MULLION	Vertical member dividing the lights of a window
NEO–CLASSICISM	Style of classical architecture and decoration prevalent in England in the late eighteenth and early nineteenth centuries, derived directly from the study of antique buildings
NEWEL POST	Central pillar of winding stair, or principal post at angle of well stair
ORMOLU	Decorative objects of cast bronze, especially mounts for furniture, chased and fire gilded
PALLADIANISM	Style of classical architecture derived from the buildings and publications of Andrea Palladio (1508–80), dominant in England from the 1720s until the ascendance of neo-classicism (qv)
PARTERRE	In a garden, a level area laid out with an ornamental, usually complex, pattern of beds and paths

PIANO NOBILE	Principal floor of a house, containing the main reception rooms, set above a basement or other subsidiary storey
PIER GLASS	Tall narrow mirror designed to hang on wall between windows
PIER TABLE	Table designed to be set between two windows, under a pier glass (qv)
PLINTH	Projecting base of a structure
PRESBYTERY	East end of a church, between choir and high altar, normally reserved for the clergy
SCAGLIOLA	Composition used to imitate marble
SCREENS PASSAGE	Passage, divided from the Great Hall by a screen, acting as the entrance to a house and separating the hall from the service rooms
SIBYL	Pagan prophetess or oracle-teller
STRING COURSE	Projecting moulding running horizontally across façade of building
STUCCO	Plasterwork, plain or decorated, executed in imitation of stonework
TRANSEPT	Transverse arm of cruciform church
TRANSOM	Horizontal member dividing lights of a window
TRIBUNE	Raised platform or gallery in a church or chapel
VESTAL	Woman of spotless chastity (i.e. devoted to the goddess Vesta)

Principal sources

Primary Sources

Audley End House, scrapbook and collection of architectural drawings
Bodleian Library, MS Top Gen e51 (R C Hussey papers)
   MS Eng Lett C223–C227 (J C Brooke/J Griffin Griffin correspondence)
   MS Gough Drawings a4, 67 (survey *c*1730)
Essex Record Office, Braybrooke archives (D/DBy, accession 5859 and temporary accession
   1974), primarily for post 1752 building history of house
Public Record Office, Works and Lord Chamberlain's accounts, for house as royal palace,
   1668–1701
Sir John Soane's Museum, John Thorpe's Book of Architecture; Adam drawings collection

Secondary Sources

Addison, W, *Audley End* (1953)
Braybrooke, Richard Lord, *The History of Audley End and Saffron Walden* (1836)
Cornforth, J, 'Victorian views of Audley End,' *Country Life*, 8 July 1976
Drury, P J, 'No other Palace in the Kingdom will compare with it'; The Evolution of
Audley End, 1605–1745', *Architectural History* 23 (1980), 1–39
Drury, P J, 'Walden Abbey into Audley End' in *Saffron Walden: Excavations and Research
1972–80* (S R Bassett) CBA Research Report 45 (1982), 94–105
Drury, P J, 'A mid eighteenth-century floor at Audley End,' *Post-Medieval Archaeology*
16 (1982), 125–140
Drury, P J, 'Joseph Rose senior's site workshop at Audley End,' *Antiquaries Journal* 64
(1984).
Mulder-Erkelens, A M L E, 'Een Hollands Scipio-Tapijt *De overgave Van Carthago* Anno
1609,' *Nederlands Kunsthistorisch Jaarboek* 31 (1980), 36–49
Tipping, H A, 'Audley End,' *Country Life* 59 (1926), pp 872, 916; 60, pp 94, 128
Tipping, H A, *English Homes, Period III, Vol II: Late Tudor and Early Stuart, 1558–1649*
(1927), 239–76
Williams, J D, *Audley End: The Restoration of 1762–97* (1966)
Williams, J D, 'The finances of an eighteenth-century Essex nobleman, *Essex Archaeol
Hist* 9 (1977), 113–28
Williams, J D, 'A pattern of land accumulation: The Audley End Experience, 1762–97,'
Essex Archaeol Hist 11 (1979), 90–100